PSTCC LIBRARY KNOXVILLE, TN

W9-AAQ-679

NEW DIRECTIONS FOR COMMUNITY COLLEGES

Arthur M. Cohen
EDITOR-IN-CHIEF

Florence B. Brawer
ASSOCIATE EDITOR

Gender and Power in the Community College

Barbara K. Townsend
University of Memphis

EDITOR

PELLISSIPPI

Number 89, Spring 1995

JOSSEY-BASS PUBLISHERS
San Francisco

ERIC®

Clearinghouse for Community Colleges

GENDER AND POWER IN THE COMMUNITY COLLEGE
Barbara K. Townsend (ed.)
New Directions for Community Colleges, no. 89
Volume XXIII, number 1
Arthur M. Cohen, Editor-in-Chief
Florence B. Brawer, Associate Editor

© 1995 by Jossey-Bass Inc., Publishers. All rights reserved.

No part of this issue may be reproduced in any form—except for a brief quotation (not to exceed 500 words) in a review or professional work—without permission in writing from the publishers.

Microfilm copies of issues and articles are available in 16mm and 35mm, as well as microfiche in 105mm, through University Microfilms Inc., 300 North Zeeb Road, Ann Arbor, Michigan 48106-1346.

LC 85-644753   ISSN 0194-3081   ISBN 0-7879-9913-X

NEW DIRECTIONS FOR COMMUNITY COLLEGES is part of The Jossey-Bass Higher and Adult Education Series and is published quarterly by Jossey-Bass Inc., Publishers, 350 Sansome Street, San Francisco, California 94104-1342 (publication number USPS 121-710) in association with the ERIC Clearinghouse for Community Colleges. Second-class postage paid at San Francisco, California, and at additional mailing offices. POST-MASTER: Send address changes to New Directions for Community Colleges, Jossey-Bass Inc., Publishers, 350 Sansome Street, San Francisco, California 94104-1342.

SUBSCRIPTIONS for 1995 cost $49.00 for individuals and $72.00 for institutions, agencies, and libraries.

THE MATERIAL in this publication is based on work sponsored wholly or in part by the Office of Educational Research and Improvement, U.S. Department of Education, under contract number RI-93-00-2003. Its contents do not necessarily reflect the views of the Department, or any other agency of the U.S. Government.

EDITORIAL CORRESPONDENCE should be sent to the Editor-in-Chief, Arthur M. Cohen, at the ERIC Clearinghouse for Community Colleges, University of California, 3051 Moore Hall, 405 Hilgard Avenue, Los Angeles, California 90024-1521.

Cover photograph © Rene Sheret, After Image, Los Angeles, California, 1990.

Manufactured in the United States of America on Lyons Falls Pathfinder Tradebook. This paper is acid-free and 100 percent totally chlorine-free.

CONTENTS

Editor's Notes

The community college is full of women. More than 50 percent of its students are women, close to half its faculty are women, and over 10 percent of community college presidents are female. What is the effect of so many women on the institution? Does their presence mean the community college operates differently than other sectors of higher education? Is there a more equitable distribution of power between men and women in the community college than in four-year colleges and universities?

The answers to these questions are not known because so little is known about women in the two-year school. As the chapters in this book indicate, there is little research about these women. They are rarely studied and they even more rarely write about themselves.

Organizational voices about women in the community college are few. The American Association of Community Colleges (AACC) has made only two official pronouncements about women in the community college. Both were in the 1970s and in the context of statements on equal opportunity and affirmative action. AACC's support of women is manifested largely through its affiliated council, the American Association of Women in Community Colleges (AAWCC), formed in 1973. The AAWCC has been active in developing women administrators through state and regional activities. The only other significant organizational voice is the National Institute for Leadership Development, supported by the AAWCC, the Maricopa Community Colleges, and the League for Innovation. Providing leadership development activities for women, the institute is the major training program for women community college leaders. Central to its approach is understanding and valuing of women's leadership styles and developing the whole person.

These efforts to develop women leaders are commendable, and may well be bearing fruit. The community college has a higher percentage of women presidents than any other institutional type. As presidents, women are in positions of power to effect change. They have the opportunity to help create and develop an institutional environment that embraces women, minorities, and all nontraditional students and staff. It is not only women presidents who have this opportunity. All institutional presidents can strive to do so. What is not clear is if the gender of a president may be a factor in that person's willingness or desire to use institutional power to develop an inclusive environment. This is but one of the questions that could be asked about the relationship between gender and power in the community college.

To examine this relationship, the authors in this book have sought to describe the situation of women in community colleges—what we know about them and what we do not—and to ascertain their influence on the two-year school and its influence on them. Authors have also speculated about what the community college might look like if women had more power in the community college.

Assumptions About Gender and Power

In putting together *Gender and Power in the Community College,* the chapter authors worked from certain assumptions about gender and power. The first assumption is that gender is socially constructed and that through gender socialization "women are acculturated into a lower power position within society" (Barge, 1994, p. 193). Gender socialization results in stereotypes that usually operate to women's disadvantage socially, politically, and economically because certain characteristics seen as feminine are viewed as less desirable than characteristics commonly viewed as masculine.

In the community college both women and men—as faculty, students, and administrators—are affected negatively by gender stereotypes. Women are not the only ones who suffer from power imbalances resulting from pervasive gender stereotypes. For example, men who sexually harass women lose some of their humanity in so doing.

Another assumption of this volume is that the power affecting gender relations within an institution is primarily structurally based. The amount of institutional power people have is defined by their position within the institutional hierarchy. Hence college presidents and vice presidents have more structural power than faculty, who have more power than students.

Those with structural power often create or maintain structural barriers to inhibit women's acquisition of power. Sometimes these actions are unwitting ones, the product of not being sufficiently sensitive to how current operating practices can harm women's opportunities for success. For example, not providing child care to students hinders the academic success of women students who may have to drop out or miss classes because they can not find babysitters.

This emphasis on structurally based power is not typical in discussions about women and power. Instead, many discussions seem to be framed by an implicit assumption that power is a characteristic of the individual and is based on personal abilities rather than on one's position within the institution. Individual empowerment within the power structure rather than collective empowerment that could also change or alter power relations and the definition of power is often stressed in this approach. For example, in *Women in the Community College* (1981), Eaton states that the community college should lead the way in the social changes involving and resulting from contemporary feminism. However, she also states that "primary responsibility for achievement rests with the individual" (p. x). This emphasis on women needing to do all the work to change society dominates writing on women in general; writings about women in the community college are no exception.

Just as individuals' power within an organization is largely a structural phenomenon, so too is an institution's power. Even though community colleges represent over 40 percent of the nation's 3,600 nonprofit higher education institutions, the community college as an institutional type has less status and consequently less power in academe than four-year colleges and universities. Being a two-year open admissions institution places it at the bottom of the institutional hierarchy. The community college's low status affects how its constituents are viewed and treated in the academy. When many faculty at four-year institutions learn some students are community college transfer students, they frequently view these students differently and assume they will be less able than students who started in the four-year college. Similarly, faculty at senior institutions often look down on two-year college faculty and do not consider them peers. Thus, discussions of gender and power for community college constituents in this volume include an awareness that the community college's status or place within the academic community as well as within society in general affects the power of its constituents.

Overview of Volume

To bring forth some of the issues about gender and power in the community college, this volume presents chapters that focus primarily on women—as students, staff, and faculty—or that illustrate situations, such as sexual harassment, in which power imbalances usually work to women's detriment.

In Chapter One, John H. Frye examines the history of the community college up to 1970 to see how women students and staff were treated and to analyze their effect on the two-year school.

In Chapter Two, Berta Vigil Laden and Caroline Sotello Viernes Turner examine the literature on women and minority students in the two-year school and illustrate how little of it focuses on women students and their needs. The authors also suggest how the community college can empower women by changing or modifying curricular programs and services and organizational structures.

In Chapter Three, Mildred García urges those in student affairs to adopt a feminist perspective that would view women's needs as central rather than peripheral to the community college.

In Chapter Four, I examine the limited literature on women two-year faculty to determine if they are operating in the mainstream or on the margins of the community college.

In Chapter Five, Nancy LaPaglia draws on her study of the representation of the two-year school in popular culture to show how this representation does an injustice to the community college's ambitious, hardworking women students and its dedicated female faculty.

In Chapter Six, Robert O. Riggs and Patricia Hillman Murrell write about the relationship between power and sexual harassment and speculate about why sexual harassment may occur less often in the community college than in other institutional types.

In Chapter Seven, Susan B. Twombly writes about how the images of leadership in the community college literature may undervalue the skills and strengths that women and minorities could bring to the college presidency because these strengths and skills are not viewed as important ones by those who write about effective faculty and leadership.

In Chapter Eight, Deborah M. DiCroce analyzes both the impact of women on the community college presidency and women's potential to make a unique contribution to this institution and to society as a whole by connecting the characteristic strengths of their gender to the power of the office. She then proposes a framework for action.

The community college needs to be responsive to changes in American society and thus responsive to the actual, not stereotypically conceived, needs of female and male students, faculty, and administrators. Being sensitive to the relationship between gender and power provides institutional leaders with an opportunity to be pathfinders in higher education.

Barbara K. Townsend
Editor

References

Barge, J. K. *Leadership: Communication Skills for Organizations and Groups*. New York: St. Martin's Press, 1994.

Eaton, J. S. "Editor's Notes." In J. S. Eaton (ed.), *Women in Community Colleges*. New Directions for Community Colleges, no. 34. San Francisco: Jossey-Bass, 1981.

BARBARA K. TOWNSEND is professor of higher education and chair of the Department of Leadership at the University of Memphis. For eight years she was a full-time faculty member, teaching developmental English and study skills, at Thomas Nelson Community College.

*The influence of women students and staff on the two-year college and
its influence on them during the years 1900 to 1970 is discussed.*

Women in the Two-Year College, 1900 to 1970

John H. Frye

In April 1949 William Boyce wrote in the *Junior College Journal* (*JCJ*) that a
"family" name was needed for the two-year college. He objected to "junior"
because of the various inferior images associated with the name. More than a
year later in the *JCJ*, James Reynolds (1950) published his well-known editorial calling for a change in name to "community college" for two-year institutions. Neither writer mentioned an earlier *JCJ* article by Catherine Robbins,
dean of women at Pasadena City College. In her February 1949 article, "Community-College Education for Women," Robbins drew on the tradition of com-
munity-based education and preparation for community life that had been a
part of the junior college rhetoric for many years. From her perspective as a
woman, the institutional name, community college, was a logical one. She saw
the community college as meeting women's goals not only for "gracious family life" and "social competence" for women, but also for "earning a living" and
offering young women "opportunities equivalent to those offered boys" (Robbins, 1949, p. 330).

   We see two important concepts exhibited in this sequence of articles.
First, a woman draws logical conclusions from the history of the two-year college and from the professional ideology of educators to create an institutional
name compatible with the perceived needs and aspirations of women. Second,
her contribution is totally ignored by male writers because her point of view
was not considered significant to an institution whose history was dominated
by men.

   As with women administrators, the literature largely ignores women students in the two-year college. However, the literature also reveals a subtle and
significant shift in the social position of women over a seventy-year period to

1970. Women changed the two-year college while the two-year college changed women. This symbiosis reflects larger changes in the general society. By their choices, women eroded curricula designed to support their traditional roles as the nurturers of men and children. And even in the limited materials available, women teachers and administrators can be seen encouraging female students to seek new realms.

Curriculum and Enrollment: The Women's Place

Several characteristics in the historical evolution of the two-year college created a favorable environment for women students. For one thing, junior college leaders, local and national, could never clearly arrive at a consensus about the mission of the two-year college (Frye, 1992). Should it be terminal or transfer or both? Which one should be emphasized? Was it for occupational training or training for citizenship or "social intelligence"? The contradictory nature of the various rationales for the junior college and the incompatibility of the actual practices of the two-year schools, as against the theory of what they should be doing, created an ambivalent environment in which student motives could be highly influential. Next, coeducation, strong in the high schools, came naturally into the junior college. Local nonresidential colleges had strong appeal to parents reluctant to send daughters to distant colleges. And not least, the two-year college emphasized growth in numbers of programs, institutions, and enrollment. Such characteristics militated against gender-based policies that would limit program enrollment based on gender and other such criteria. The result was a relatively welcoming atmosphere for women students even if the male-dominated culture burdened women enrollees with limited visibility.

For some writers the issue of women's place was a pressing one. Early in the twentieth century, one writer defined the role of women as the "social trinity of wife, mother, and member of society" (Eschbach, 1993, p. 170). The facts were clear by 1900, however, that women's place in paid work was increasing and likely to continue to increase. There may have been many men and some women educators in the twentieth century who still held to the cult of true womanhood, viewed as dependence on men, passivity, and sexual purity, but this language is conspicuously absent from the educational literature, and no writer went to the extreme of advocating excluding women from the work force.

The special place of women in raising children, maintaining a home life, and carrying the values of culture has remained consistent. From the "social trinity" already noted to the most recent feminist literature, women are seen as having special and critical skills. Hulbert and Schuster's 1993 book on educated women argues that "networks of relationships and responsibilities" are a "central organizing element in women's lives" (p. 421) in contrast to the individualism, competitiveness, and aggressiveness of men. Although some contemporary feminists insist on absolute gender equality in access to education, even considering those differences just noted, earlier educators were not so certain the logical outcome of these differences was to provide the same educational program to men and women.

One 1930 author in Kent's *Higher Education in America* (1930) suggested the women would need to have reduced general education requirements so the necessary courses in homemaking could be managed. In 1949 Eckert, consultant to the California Department of Education, wrote a *JCJ* article to promote "family life guidance" (p. 27). He noted the rising divorce rate, delinquency, and other family problems that called for the junior college to provide guidance to solve these social problems. If women were to be trained for careers and for homemaking while men were trained only for careers, there was a problem in curriculum. So the argument went. Access to education presented the problem of providing for women's special role in society.

The process of resolving this issue in an open access college was further complicated by women students' choices. Whatever programs were provided or whatever theories drove the program, women, like men, tended to choose programs that met their self-determined needs and flagrantly ignored the most painfully reasoned educational arguments about these needs.

In a 1941 *JCJ* article on terminal education several young women were interviewed about their reasons for enrolling in the two-year college. Their responses are instructive, if not surprising. One indicated that she attended the junior college to gain "my life career." (Why I Am Enrolled in a Terminal Curriculum," p. 558). Later she assertively expressed her goals by telling the interviewer, "When I reach my goal in life, and I will. . . ." Another whose aim was personnel work noted a college education was "the one thing I wanted above all" (p. 558). Her career plans benefited from a scholarship from the Morgan Park Women's Club.

A third young woman was not "satisfied with myself" without college ("Why I Am Enrolled in a Terminal Curriculum," 1941, p. 560). She went on to observe that one girl in her class was studying so she could be a greater help to her male employer who did not have strong English skills and another girl did not want her children to surpass her intellectually. Other women expressed the need for intellectual companionship or noted that most of the men they worked for had college degrees. The implication was that the "girls" needed to be comfortable in the presence of their bosses. Another said her education was necessary to gain "the highest position any of our young women can hope to reach" in her particular firm (p. 566).

These responses reveal both initiative and ambition and, at the same time, a relatively passive acceptance of the status quo. In this respect the responses mirror the general ambivalence that characterizes the attitude toward women in the junior college literature and in the United States as a whole before World War II.

The fly in the ointment, as Kluckhohn has argued (Kiell and Friedman, 1957), was that because the highest social status adheres to successful competitive individualism, women are not likely to limit their aspirations to an ideal of womanhood that necessarily forgoes this opportunity for the highest rewards. The tendency in the educational literature to grant women more and more leeway in their career aspirations is a noticeable trend, especially among the women writers we discuss later, and this speaks to Kluckhohn's insight.

Courses for Women

Instructional programs specifically for women were of two kinds. For one, there were traditional occupations for women such as health care, secretarial work, and teaching. Another group of courses was vocational in a different sense, that is, courses in homemaking or family life.

The nurturing, caring qualities attributed to women were thought to be appropriate to health fields. For example, the Dental Hygiene Association published a promotional brochure, "The Dental Hygienist: A Career for Women" (Stoll, 1945). Also, state laws apparently restricted this occupational field to women (Stoll, 1945). Secretarial fields were dominated by women and even many graduates of the better four-year colleges engaged in secretarial or related office work. One report on the junior college secretarial program boasted of the success rates of its graduates and apparently saw no irony in the role that relatives played in finding work for graduates, "particularly by stepping into (their) fathers' offices" (Thompson, 1940, p. 201). Not only does this suggest the elevated social class of female junior college students in 1940, but illustrates the low social expectations for women in the work force. Families understood paid careers for women to be largely matters of providing support until marriage and family.

Although nursing and secretarial programs were almost exclusively enrolled in by women, teacher education was not. One two-year college boasted of a course for prospective teachers and the parity between male and female enrollment. However, one of the training films used was *Our Teacher, Mary Dean* (Aumack and Siemens, 1950). Education curricula were popular with both women and men students. Outside of California where education courses were prohibited in junior colleges, nearly half the occupational students were enrolled in education (Frye, 1992). Robert Pedersen suggested that normal schools drew large numbers of female students away from the two-year college when the two were geographically proximate (personal communication, April 1994).

From the perspective of those who promoted terminal education in the junior college, home economics appeared to be an ideal course of study for women, who would then take up their place in the home as pillars of society while men did the world's business. Like so many programs associated with two-year terminal education, this one failed. Eells (1941) reported that only 9 percent of the women students enrolled in junior college home economics courses. By 1950, of 400 colleges surveyed, only 99 offered family life courses and 44 of those were in private junior colleges whose enrollment was undergoing rapid decline (Martorana, 1948). Home economics courses also tended to take on a more theoretical and academic orientation in time. This was an attempt by its professoriate to gain academic status in the university. This attempt largely failed and did little to increase women's enrollment in the field (Hoffschwelle, 1991).

Courses in family life, marriage education, family relations, and community service, originally aimed at the special place of women, both declined in popularity and changed their emphasis just as home economics had done. One course touted in the *JCJ* boasted that none of its graduates had, as far as was known, ended in divorce court (Squires, 1941). Squires further illustrated the contribution of this course by describing a situation in which a young woman was dissuaded from marrying a man from a different religious background. Such thinking reveals the social control assumptions behind such courses (as well as some less respectable assumptions).

Writers attempted to promote such courses by praising the demanding role of homemaker in community life. There was much talk about women's community leadership roles in school and church. By 1960 some authors were insisting on more family education because women were working outside the home more and more. The implication was that training in housekeeping skills was more needed because women were spending less time there as they spent more time in the work force (Gambill, 1960). The claim was made that students were demanding such courses, although no supporting evidence was provided.

What tended to happen to such courses over time was that they were transformed from courses with a terminal intent to courses based on academic disciplines whose basic purpose was transfer. Courses on family life were replaced by ones titled "Sociology of the Family" and "Child Psychology." This trend repeats the pattern in home economics where the original focus was lost as the elements of scholarly discipline replaced the social control elements of the earlier purpose. Although study of the community and women's role as leaders in solving community problems was often a part of the early family and marriage programs in two-year colleges, by 1960 courses on community issues tended to focus on large-scale social solutions such as the United Nations and regional planning. The sense of training women to provide local community leadership had been almost completely lost (Kelly, 1966).

In an unusual article that appears to have attracted little attention, Cooke (1933) noted that women's role in trades and industry was being completely ignored by the junior college. He cited census data to show that women worked in trades and industrial occupations at precisely the same percentage as did men, or about one-third of all women employed. Cooke concluded that trades training should be made equally available for women for this reason.

Cooke's view appeared to make no headway. Most writers about the two-year college persisted in seeing its female students from a traditional perspective that stressed their role as homemakers and community volunteers. The response of many women students was not to enroll in programs that exemplified this traditional domestic role. By their enrollment patterns, women revolutionized the concept of women's education. Women ignored the traditional vision of their role and sought college programs that would enhance their economic and professional opportunities rather than limit them. In other words, women students appear to have killed through benign neglect the college programs that exemplified the traditional role of women.

Administrative Leadership: Women's Place in Program and Policy

Before 1970, female leaders in the community college movement were few and far between. Women presidents of two-year colleges appear to be marginal figures nationally. Deans of women are the one collective exception to the lack of women in policy positions. Male domination of administrative positions was not obvious because it was taken for granted. A 1960 profile of junior college presidents does not even mention gender (Hawk, 1960). A 1953 article by Pierce on the growing trend to establish offices of academic dean as second in command to the president could find only two women nationwide in such a position. In Pierce's survey, 86 percent of the replies indicated "men as preferred" for this high office. The first personality trait presidents looked for in their second in command was "loyalty" (p. 293). The overriding importance of personal loyalty and subordination to the president is obvious. In 1951 it must have been difficult for males to conceive of a woman in such a powerful and intimate position in relation to the president. Clearly it was difficult for the presidents.

If women were absent from positions of power, does it follow they were powerless and lacked influence on the evolution of the two-year college? As sparse as the evidence is, there is reason to believe this was not the case. The very ambiguity of the two-year college mission provided a rhetoric that was amenable to interpretation and influence by women even in subordinate positions within the institutions. A politically sophisticated ideology of feminism is not necessary for women to make incremental choices that have the effect of improving opportunities for their gender. As we saw in this chapter's introductory section about naming the community college, women could very well make connections between their vision of the "community" college and their gendered needs, even if men were blind to the implications or simply indifferent to them.

The Movement for Student Development and Women in the Two-Year College

Some evidence indicates that women deans and counselors in the two-year college had a cumulative and incremental effect in changing the paradigm by which women were viewed and by which they viewed themselves. In one of those suggestive brief notices that commonly appear in the early issues of the JCJ, Stuelke (1945), dean of women at Fullerton Junior College, spoke of the role of the woman dean in "What Does a Dean Do?" Significantly, this brief notice was republished in the JCJ from its first appearance in the Fullerton News-Tribune, the local newspaper. Stuelke writes that the dean of women directs "the energies of young women into channels of real education." She describes a hypothetical situation in which a young female student wants to organize a war bond drive. The dean, Stuelke says, helps the young women organize the drive with the result of thousands of dollars in bonds sold, "but, more important for education, a leader who through initiative and experience has prepared herself for active citizenship," an example, we are to understand, of "real education." Other examples are a "social evening" for Marines or a special edition of the student newspaper to be sent to "service men and women" overseas. The result, Stuelke says, is "a social consciousness aroused in the young woman" (Stuelke, 1945, p. 423).

Stuelke also lists concerns that young women bring to her office. "How can I be sure . . . [my] credits . . . will be accepted at Berkeley or Stanford?" "Am I better fitted to become a librarian or a newspaper woman?" "Should I take nurses training to help in the war effort or continue my educational plans . . .?" "Should I take a good job now or continue with my education?" (p. 424). The dean's job, says Stuelke, "is to be counsellor, guide, and friend to every woman in college" (p. 424).

Stuelke's language is far from militantly feminist, but she clearly has no intention of thrusting women into homemaking. In this respect her approach to the deanship presages the self-conscious feminism enunciated by Truex (1971) nearly thirty years later. In a 1971 article in the *Journal of the National Association of Women Deans and Counselors,* Truex urges women to take advantage of the feminist movement to strengthen their role in college decision making. She notes that much of the association's growth was coming from the junior colleges. Stuelke's example illustrates the influence of counseling and the perspective on student development that was emerging in the first half of the twentieth century.

The history of higher education in the twentieth century reveals a strong shift in conceptualizing the function of education from training for social needs to individual student development. Terminology shifts from "social control" in the early years of the century through advising and counseling to student development by mid-century. In Kent's *Higher Education in America* (1930), J. B. Johnson of the University of Minnesota writes that the purpose of higher education should be in "terms of the self-realization of its students" (Johnson, 1930, p. 419). College is the "agency . . . [in which] the individual finds the place in life for which his innate character best fits him" (pp. 457–459). In spite of the male pronouns, nothing in his perspective could be used to exclude women. In another chapter, "Curriculum for Women," Wilkins (1930), president of Oberlin College, wrote, "No reasonable person in this day and generation would think of limiting women's interests to the home, or of denying them full access to all human knowledge and experience" (pp. 457–458). Although this statement may be prescriptive rather than descriptive, the trend is clearly articulated.

This perspective is strongly expressed in the general literature of higher education and the junior college as well. The *JCJ* published a long review of Cassidy and Kozman's 1947 *Counseling Girls in a Changing Society.* The reviewer,

Meinecke (1949), a dean at Colby Junior College in New Hampshire, quotes extensively from the book. "The end goal of a woman's life in our democracy" should be to create a "'responsible co-worker with man, for the good of human beings and the society in which she lives, rather than that of a dependent inferior, holding someone else responsible for her and for her support'" (p. 274). Continuing, Meinecke writes that a woman's role should be "as a partner of man, rather than a competitor or a subordinate, in all relationships . . ." and that the most important of four "developmental tasks" of the adolescent girl is to "understand and accept a new self" (1949, p. 274).

This more liberal view of women's education grows to dominate the literature, but it coexists with the more traditional view of women that homemaking and motherhood are the primary duties to be expected. However, although there is little specifically on counseling women (Durnall and Reichart, 1954), incidental references make clear that counselors and advisers relate to women in ways that are less and less traditional. Girls were demanding "a changed social order" (Sisson, 1934).

Although males dominated the two-year college, and the tendency to view women as subordinate and as future homemakers persisted strongly (and still continues), the powerful desire for institutional growth prevented any conservative tendency from pushing programs to limit women's options. Although it is likely that the male leadership's insensitivity to women's issues retarded the development of structures and programs favorable to women, leaders' desire for growth in enrollment would make active support of restrictive policies and programming a self-defeating choice. In the face of this situation the growing consciousness of deans of women, women counselors, and women teachers could exert an important influence on female students and on policies and practices of institutions.

Conclusion: Are We "Oppressors or Liberators"?

Truex (1971) asked women administrators and counselors if they were the "oppressors or liberators" of today's college women (p. 18). This brief survey of women in the two-year college before 1970 reveals an institution in which local and national leadership is almost entirely male dominated but also an institution whose ill-defined mission allows for contradictory rhetorical emphases. This ambivalence is exacerbated by an ideology that increasingly emphasizes opportunity, individual development, and ready access for all people including women. These qualities were strengthened by the leadership's desire to promote enrollment and institutional growth. The openness and flexibility, which might have opened revolutionary tendencies in women's education, appears to have been counterbalanced by a profound and fundamental indifference to women's issues by the male-dominated leadership. Although a substantial number of women served as professionals in the two-year college, there is little evidence of conscious feminism.

Whether this conservatism resulted from institutional limitations experienced by women professionals or broader social factors is unclear. The dynamic force for change regarding women in the two-year college is clearly seen in how women students make choices. Women's choices killed home economics, women enrolled in increasing numbers in disciplines traditionally labeled male, and they left no uncertainty in the minds of deans of women that their interests were changing.

How can we determine the impact of the two-year college on women, their aspirations and their futures? Qualitative as well as quantitative studies will be essential. Individual histories of female students will be important. The intentions of families in supporting females in college will be critical. Do families think girls need jobs until marriage? Is there fear of divorce and death of the spouse? Do families and spouses increasingly expect women to work after or during child rearing as well as before? What do the women themselves foresee?

In addition to students, female administrators in the two-year college need serious analysis. For example, how did the social backgrounds of female staff differ from male staff in the two-year college, if at all? Did women staff come to the two-year college because it offered a career when their male counterparts had higher expectations and more success in achieving their aspirations? If true, what effect did this have on women professionals and what they said to and did for their female students? And if it is true that women professionals in the two-year college were generally conservative in terms of their approaches to feminism before 1970, what happened to this group after 1970 and what has been their impact?

It is undoubtedly true that between 1900 and 1970 many more women went to college than would have had the two-year college not been created. But this does not answer the question of what effect this institution had on the life courses of women students. This question is important not only for the history of women in the United States but it is important as well for understanding the interrelationships between institutions and individuals and groups within American society.

References

Aumack, G., and Siemens, C. H. "Exploring Teaching as a Career with Junior College Students." *Junior College Journal*, Oct. 1950, pp. 72–75.

Boyce, W. "Wanted: A Family Name." *Junior College Journal*, Apr. 1949, pp. 440–445.

Cooke, R. L. "Industrial Training of Junior College Women." *Junior College Journal*, Dec. 1933, pp. 116–120.

Durnall, E. J., Jr., and Reichart, R. R. "Student Personnel Practices in Junior Colleges for Women." *Junior College Journal*, Sept. 1954, pp. 41–45.

Eckert, R. G. "Wanted: Family Life Guidance in the Junior College." *Junior College Journal*, Sept. 1949, pp. 27–30.

Eells, W. C. *Why Junior College Terminal Education.* Washington, D.C.: American Association of Junior Colleges, 1941.

Eschbach, E. S. *The Higher Education of Women in England and America, 1865–1920.* New York: Garland, 1993.

Frye, J. H. *The Vision of the Public Junior College, 1900–1940.* New York: Greenwood Press, 1992.

Gambill, G. W. "Historical Background of Marriage Education." *Junior College Journal,* Dec. 1960, pp. 225–228.

Hawk, R. "A Profile of Junior College Presidents." *Junior College Journal,* Feb. 1960, pp. 340–346.

Hoffschwelle, M. S. "The Science of Domesticity: Home Economics at George Peabody College for Teachers, 1914–1939." *The Journal of Southern History,* 1991, 57 (4), 659–680.

Hulbert, K., and Schuster, D. *Women's Lives Through Time.* San Francisco: Jossey-Bass, 1993.

Johnson, J. B. "Selection of Students." In R. Kent (ed.), *Higher Education in America.* Boston: Ginn, 1930.

Kelly, M. F. "Finding the Community in Community College." *Junior College Journal,* Nov. 1966, pp. 26–27.

Kent, R. A. (ed.). *Higher Education in America.* Boston: Ginn, 1930.

Kiell, N., and Friedman, B. "Culture Lag and Housewifemanship: The Role of the Married Female College Graduate." *Journal of Educational Sociology,* 1957, 31 (2), 87–95.

Martorana, S. V. "Functional Family-Life Education in Junior Colleges." *Junior College Journal,* Oct. 1948, pp. 79–88.

Meinecke, C. D. "Review of Rosalind Cassidy and Hilda Clute Kozman, Counseling Girls in a Changing Society: A Guide for Counselors and Teachers in High School and College." *Junior College Journal,* Jan. 1949, pp. 272–275. Quoting Cassidy, R., and Kozman, C. *Counseling Girls in a Changing Society.* New York: McGraw-Hill, 1947.

Pierce, A. C. "Junior College Deans: Their Qualifications and Training." *Junior College Journal,* Mar. 1953, pp. 293–394.

Reynolds, J. W. "What Is a Community College?" *Junior College Journal,* Dec. 1950, pp. 201–202.

Robbins, C. J. "Community-College Education for Women." *Junior College Journal,* Feb. 1949, pp. 330–332.

Sisson, E. I. "Regulations in Private Colleges for Women." *Junior College Journal,* May 1934, pp. 414–417.

Squires, J. D. "Guidance Toward Marriage and Family Life." *Junior College Journal,* Mar. 1941, pp. 387–391.

Stoll, F. A. "The Dental Hygienist." *Junior College Journal,* Feb. 1945, pp. 253–255.

Stuelke, M. V. "What Does a Dean Do?" *Junior College Journal,* May 1945, pp. 423–424.

Thompson, W. H. "Secretarial Science Graduates of Colby." *Junior College Journal,* Dec. 1940, pp. 200–203.

Truex, D. "Education of Women, the Student Personnel Profession, and the New Feminism." *Journal of the National Association of Women Deans and Counselors,* Fall 1971, pp. 13–20.

"Why I Am Enrolled in a Terminal Curriculum: A Symposium by Students of Illinois Junior Colleges." *Junior College Journal,* May 1941, pp. 558–566.

Wilkins, E. "The College Curriculum." In R. Kent (ed.), *Higher Education in America.* Boston: Ginn, 1930.

JOHN H. FRYE is instructor of history at Triton College in River Grove, Illinois.

Ignored in most research, women students, particularly those of color,
remain an invisible majority in community colleges.

Viewing Community College Students Through the Lenses of Gender and Color

Berta Vigil Laden, Caroline Sotello Viernes Turner

In the fall of 1985 the young Chicana sat in a chair in the community college counselor's office. Her name was Sylvia. Her face lit up and her gestures became quite animated as she briefly told her life story to the counselor:

> I work as a clerk in an office nearby and I want to get a bachelor's degree in business administration. I grew up in the Central Valley [in California] following the crops with my parents. My mother has always been an inspiration. She set up a little business, a store, after my father could no longer pick crops, and she made it successful. She always told us that we should make the very best of any situation as she did. After finishing high school, I got married and worked while my husband went to college and then on to law school. On the day he graduated from law school, with no warning, he told me goodbye and left. Fortunately, we had no children. I continued working and recently began taking business classes here at the college. My boss is encouraging me to go on to the university and get my bachelor's degree. I want to find out what courses I need to take to transfer to San Jose State in business administration. My company will help me with tuition and books as long as I continue to work there. I work full time so I can only take classes after work, which I have been doing for over a year. My teachers here are very supportive as is my boss. Coming to class is enjoyable for me even though I take two evening classes and still have to go home and do homework after a long day at work.

Two and half years later, Sylvia had enough credits to transfer into a selective business administration program at the University of California, Berkeley. She also received a chancellor's scholarship. In addition, after several promotions at work, she had been asked to stay on in a part-time capacity with an offer to work her schedule around her classes. However, Sylvia decided to move to Berkeley and find a campus job. Staying at her present job would only prolong the time it would take her to complete the bachelor's degree requirements. In June 1989 Sylvia graduated from UC Berkeley with honors and was encouraged by a college dean to apply for the MBA program. A letter to her community college counselor stated:

> I know I would never have considered going to UC Berkeley if you had not encouraged me and seen the potential in me that I did not see in myself. Now I want to work for a while in financial planning, then apply to the MBA program in a few years. Also, I hope to help other young Chicano students, especially women, go to college and get their bachelor's degrees as you, my boss, and others like you helped me. I want other women to get the kind of confidence and a sense of accomplishment I have gained from going to college and the joy of learning I have experienced. (Sylvia is a pseudonym for a student interviewed by Laden [1990].)

Sylvia's story is not an uncommon one for many women community college students. Many are working full time, many are raising a family, and many are single parents. In this chapter, we examine the community college literature as it relates to the experience of women community college students like Sylvia. We are particularly interested in literature that examines issues for women of color.

What Does the Research Literature Say About Women Students?

Not only are more women students enrolling in community colleges and completing more of the associate degrees, Long and Blanchard (1991) argue that this population now "constitute[s] the new majority in most degree programs from associate degrees to graduate degrees with few exceptions" (p. 47). In light of women's increasing college-going participation and associate degree completion, to what degree has the role of women students been addressed in the community college literature? The answer might be summed up in two words: not much. Well-known works that include an examination of the community college and its students (Brint and Karabel, 1989; Cohen and Brawer, 1987, 1989; Cross, 1971) and students of color in higher education (Astin, 1988; Richardson and Bender, 1987) do not address the diversity among women community college students. Ethnic women are not discussed as a separate group by Astin until the conclusion of his study where some specific recommendations are offered. Even these recommendations are geared generally to all women of color in colleges and universities rather than specifying that different needs may exist for women students by racial/ethnic group in two- and four-year colleges, respectively.

In *The Dilemma of Access: Minorities in Two Year Colleges,* Olivas (1979) addresses the role and impact of race and ethnicity in the community college. Olivas was one of the first researchers to document that the public two-year colleges enroll the largest concentration of minority students, and that large numbers of minority students do not persist to the associate or baccalaureate degree. In his discussion of persistence rates, Olivas underscores the fact that retention strategies may need to differ by race/ethnicity and gender. However, although he differentiates persistence rates by race and gender, most of his discussion on student characteristics presents an aggregate picture for various ethnic/racial groups. Nonetheless, Olivas's work is a milestone in addressing the issues of race and ethnicity in the community college literature.

A recent comprehensive review of the extant literature on minorities in community colleges discusses theoretically based research that tested variables affecting minority student persistence and transfer. Nora provides a thorough review of the literature on community college enrollments, student educational aspirations, the transfer function, student persistence in community college, financial aid issues, and degree attainment after transfer (Nora, 1993). He concludes with a typology of intervention strategies and policy recommendations found to be associated with minority student retention and persistence.

Nora's review provides further evidence of the continued omission of theoretical studies that focus specifically on minority women students. Nora does include a reference to one study of enrollment patterns in math and science with results reported by student gender and ethnicity. He also refers to a study by Chacon, Cohen, and Strover (1986), "Chicanos and Chicanas: Barriers to Progress in Higher Education." Nora discusses the study at the aggregate level of analysis for Chicano students but does not delineate distinctions by gender. Chacon, Cohen, and Strover (1986), however, explicitly state that the question to be addressed in their study was, "Do Chicanas (Mexican American females) encounter certain barriers related to their sex as well as obstacles stemming from their membership in an oppressed minority?" (p. 296). The Chacon, Cohen, and Strover study was the first to document the impact of domestic labor (the number of hours spent on child care, care of the elderly, cooking, cleaning, and so forth) on college program progress for Chicanas, especially for Chicanas enrolled in the community college. They state that "women put in many more hours of domestic labor than men. And domestic labor had a . . . negative impact on program progress" (p. 312). In not highlighting the significant findings of this study by gender, Nora rendered invisible the experience of the women community college students of color in this work.

In another broad discussion of community college students of color, "Degree Achievement by Minorities in Community College," Cohen (1988) provides demographic data, a discussion of the difficulties inherent in defining transfer rate, and a review of related literature. Most of the data and citations reviewed, as with other works, treat students of color in the aggregate, with few distinctions by gender.

Thus, although the study of community college students by race/ethnicity and gender appears as a growing emphasis in the community college literature, the study of women students of color in the two-year college remains sparse. Some of the recent work described in the following section provide what we call transition or bridging pieces. We now briefly review this literature beginning with research that includes some discussion of community college women and then direct our attention to works on women of color in the community college.

Gaps in the Literature

Literature on community college students is an emerging continuum: from a focus on community college students as a fairly homogeneous population to studies that begin to look at women students to studies which examine women students of color. Studies on women community college students range from those that briefly mention women students as a discrete category worthy of some separate analysis to in-depth analysis and some literature that focuses specifically on women. Most of the literature, however, focuses on white women, often classified as reentry students.

In an edited volume, Eaton (1981) provides the first work we found that is dedicated exclusively to the subject of women in community colleges. Eaton and others provide data about the impact of the changing role of women in society on the educational process in the community colleges. The topics examine women's roles within the organization as college president and in other administrative positions, as faculty members, and as members of boards of trustees, but not as students. Although several chapters are devoted to the discussion of the effects of the humanities curriculum, occupational programs, and support services on women students, women students are not discussed per se as holistic individuals. For example, a discussion of women interested in transfer and in pursuit of the bachelor's degree is noticeably absent. Although Eaton's work acknowledges the roles and activities of women in the dynamic and complicated structures of community colleges, the lack of direct attention to women students is a significant omission in the study.

A study by Twombly (1993) reviews community college research articles published between 1970 and 1989 to obtain insight into the dominant modes of thinking about women in community colleges. The low degree of interest in conducting research on women in community colleges is revealed in Twombly's typology of 174 published articles analyzed for the study. Of particular note for this chapter are two findings. One is that very few of the studies were authored by community college writers. The second finding is that of the 116 articles (66 percent) written about students, only about a half dozen dealt specifically with the topic of race and ethnicity. This latter finding is a reminder of how little research has been done on community college student populations examining issues of race/ethnicity and gender combined. Twombly urges the importance of examining the intersection of gender, race/ethnicity, and class. She notes that this lack of focus in the literature is inexcusable particularly "in a sector that serves so many women and members of minority groups" (Twombly, 1993 p. 194).

Both as a community college faculty member of many years and as a researcher, LaPaglia (1994) draws on a variety of women student experiences to examine the real-life images of community colleges as compared to fictional descriptions in popular culture. Although her focus is not on examining women of color, one-third of the women students whose journals she examines are African American and Hispanic. Their journal entries depict women leading thoughtful, active lives, making plans to reach goals, and attempting to gain some control over their lives. Their successes are attributed to support programs and services that help mitigate the stresses in their daily lives, the teachers who reach out to them and provide positive in-class and out-of-class experiences for them, and the community college itself.

In a study on low-income white women, Gittell (1986) noted that community college women students were more dependent on financial aid than men students. Gittell found that the more women students were treated like traditional students and their particular needs ignored by the community colleges, the more likely they were to drop out. Achieving academic success in college for these students was attributed to smaller classes, attention to improving basic skills and study habits, more flexible class scheduling, more attention to financial aid, on-campus child care, more sympathetic teachers and counselors, peer group support systems, and nontraditional programs to address the underlying problem of sex stereotyping in the curriculum and in advisement. Of greater concern was the seemingly routine channeling of women into demanding vocational programs with rigid course and time scheduling, restrictive course requirements, few liberal arts courses, and limited opportunities to transfer. Moreover, data Gittell examined on majors by gender distribution demonstrated that women were concentrated at the bottom end in business and health programs.

Feiger's (1991) study, entitled *The American Community College Woman*, presents an extensive review of studies that focused on reentry women. Many of the sample groups studied were white women, often from lower middle to upper middle socioeconomic levels. Most of the studies reviewed by Feiger were undertaken in the 1980s. They examine the complexity of women's roles and their attempts to balance these many roles successfully while going to college. For example, one study compares reentry women to reentry men and reveals, unsurprisingly, that most of the reentry men students who are fathers do not mention family demands as a challenge to their educational experience. However, women who are mothers mention great difficulty in combining their role as students with their familial roles, such as taking care of their children. Other studies discussed by Feiger emphasize differences between married and single women students and their fears and expectations about attending college.

Feiger (1991) also examined the influence of age, ethnicity, high school grade point average, and ages of children still living at home in describing how women students experience their community college education. Two sets of data were used: a national project using a cross-sectional survey of 7,558 students, with a distribution of 58 percent women and 26 percent ethnic minorities; and two group interviews with a total of 28 women students (15 of the 28 were women of color) in two Los Angeles community colleges. She found significant changes in community college demographics over the last decade that reflect a much greater diversity among the women student population.

Feiger also confirmed previous research findings indicating that barriers continue to exist for all women students attending community college, but particularly for adult women students with multiple sets of external responsibilities. Women with younger children experienced more barriers than women with older children; however, lack of money and insufficient time to study continue to be common concerns for all women. Finding time to study was the most frequently cited barrier and one that kept women from attending full time, especially Native American and Hispanic women. Inadequate finances were also frequently cited as a reason for taking fewer courses, especially among Asian and Hispanic women. Younger women (19 years or younger) experienced more academic pressures than more mature women, and Hispanic women experienced the most of all ethnic groups. Less than 50 percent of the sample population used student services. Less than 20 percent of the women were enrolled in academic majors or vocational programs still considered nontraditional for women; business appeared to be the most popular major.

In sum, Feiger's findings suggest that many of the barriers women faced in the 1970s and 1980s have not receded in the early 1990s. In addition, the selection of major and career choices in more nontraditional fields still remains low. Feiger concludes, "The good news, though, is that women students are still coming to college regardless of the barriers and they represent more diverse ethnic and age groups than ever. Their continuing presence may force long overdue institutional changes" (1991, p. 80).

In "A Place for Women?" Gittell (1986) strongly questioned the lack of attention being given by community colleges to their majority population—the nearly 60 percent women enrolled in community colleges across the country. She notes that urban community colleges enroll unusually high numbers of women and minority students and that the profile of urban community college women students is similar to nontraditional students entering four-year urban colleges. Interviews with 95 women of color (not distinguished in the study by racial/ethnic background) in three cities revealed their academic preparation was inadequate and many had traumatic high school experiences that led to dropping out. Nonetheless, their aspirations for higher education were high, but most faced pressing problems related to finances. Basic needs centered around financial support to attend college, child care, and medical services for their families.

Not only are there few research studies and articles available that deal comprehensively with women community college students, there are even fewer that encompass gender together with race, ethnicity, and class. We now turn our discussion to a few studies that focus on community college women students of color.

What Does the Literature Say About Women Students of Color?

Although many of the studies already discussed in this chapter include women of color in their samples, few emphasize the experience of women by racial/ethnic group. The following studies look at the community college student experience for specific racial/ethnic groups.

Hispanic Women Students. Hispanic students are the most highly concentrated groups of students in community colleges and among the most underrepresented in four-year institutions. Moreover, at least 56 percent of all Hispanic college students enroll in community colleges (Carter and Wilson, 1993). Hispanic women account for the largest percentage of this group enrolled in higher education (Carter and Wilson, 1994). The following studies have a primary focus on the experiences of Hispanic women community college students.

As noted earlier, a study by Chacon, Cohen, and Strover (1986) examined the program progress of Chicano and Chicana students enrolled in five California collegiate institutions. Females of Mexican descent comprised the majority of the study's subject pool, although it included a small sample of males for comparison at three of the five study sites. The study focused on degree completion and its relationship to barriers encountered by Hispanic students, Chicanas in particular. Sites included one community college, two state universities, a highly selective public university campus, and an elite private university. Findings reveal that the effect of gender on program progress was entirely indirect; nonetheless, Chicanas attending community college were more likely than Chicanos to experience every one of the barriers impeding program progress. Age was a factor in that the older the women, the less academically prepared and the less career guidance they appeared to have received in high school. Also, the need to perform many hours of domestic labor in the home and to work a high number of paid hours had strong negative effects on women's program progress and their academic performance. In effect, the more hours they worked in the home or on the job, the less units they were able to take. Although parental support was found to be similar for both men and women, Chicanas were more likely to report less parental support to pursue a college degree. Higher levels of stress were reported by women, particularly regarding their sense of feeling academically underprepared although their reported collegiate grade point averages were higher than the men's. Lack of money was another reported source of stress for Chicanas and may have influenced their working more hours and taking less units than Chicanos.

In her essay, "From the Barrio to the Academy: Revelations of a Mexican American Scholarship Girl," Rendon (1992) offers personal insights based on her experiences in Texas and Michigan of what it is like for Hispanic women who are often the first in their families to go to college. Rendon shares the pain and conflict and the cultural transformation she underwent in the process of going from high school to community college, transferring to a major research university for undergraduate and graduate studies, and ultimately becoming a university professor. Rendon describes her educational experiences and struggles as a young woman coping with academic life and the difficult separation from her Mexican American family and culture. In part, her experiences could be those of many other first-generation college students coming from diverse cultural and ethnic backgrounds. Although her parents were very supportive and made many sacrifices themselves to help their daughter achieve her dream of getting a college degree, Rendon notes they often did not know or understand the ordeal she was undergoing, especially after she transferred to another community college far from home. Rather, when her parents heard the pain and exhaustion in their daughter's voice on the telephone, they offered their protection the best way they knew how by offering words of encouragement to come home and leave the suffering behind: "Vente, hija. Ya deja todo eso" (p. 59). The lack of minority faculty and administrators to act as leaders, role models, and mentors only added to the alienation she felt, so that at times her parents' offer was very tempting. The small number or complete absence of individuals of color in roles of leadership and authority is still a dilemma that ethnic minority students continue to encounter in too many community colleges.

Laden (1994) examined the transfer function for Hispanic students in California. Laden's study is a qualitative/quantitative study of first-year, first-generation, primarily Mexican American, community college students interested in transfer. Her examination of transcripts indicated that although Chicanas enrolled in more units than Chicanos, on average they completed fewer units each term regardless of their age. Obligations to the family, child-care problems, transportation, and financial concerns were primary reasons for women to drop courses, take incompletes, or fail courses. The strong desire to improve their lives, however, led many of these women to reenroll the following term as full- or near full-time students, often retaking the courses they had dropped or failed. Women who were receiving financial aid and were part of a support program for low-income students that offered additional assistance for child care completed more units than those who were not involved in such programs. Extended child care also allowed the women to stay on campus after classes to study individually or in study groups and to attend tutoring sessions sponsored by the program. These findings confirm other research (Carter and

Wilson, 1994; Chacon, Cohen, and Strover, 1986; Feiger, 1991; LaPaglia, 1994; Stein, 1992; Weis, 1992) that women are still expected to be the primary caretakers of their families.

In another study with a focus on females of Mexican descent, Turner (1984) examined the process by which Hispanic community college students move toward transfer from the two- to the four-year college based on four in-depth case studies of two Hispanic females and two non-Hispanic white females who aspired to transfer. They were attending a large California community college known for its high transfer rates, particularly among its non-minority students. Turner assessed the communication network patterns by which students obtained general information on the community college they wanted to attend and specific information on the community college transfer process. The evolution of these network patterns acquired prior to and during their community college experience was documented. Linkages with the counseling center were emphasized because it was considered the formal source of transfer information at that campus.

Using a framework of basic analytic network relationships, Turner found some distinct linkage differences between the Hispanic and non-Hispanic white women students in the study. The Hispanic women students began with a distant link or no evident link to a community college counselor. During their college experience a network pattern evolved that brought the Hispanic students into a second-order relationship with the counselor such as through a friend of a friend referral. In other words, their network pattern was linked to the informal rather than to the formal transfer information flow of the community college. For the white women students, however, linkages with the campus began prior to enrolling through efforts to obtain initial information. Once on campus, they then established formal relationships with counselors who put them into the formalized transfer information flow of the institution. The key element connecting Hispanic women formally with the counseling center appeared to be through a referral from the multicultural center. Differences in the network patterns and communication links established by the Hispanic and non-Hispanic white women suggested different academic outcomes. At the end of two years, Hispanic women had taken fewer transfer courses and were less prepared to transfer than their non-Hispanic white counterparts.

Asian Women Students. Asians, a rapidly escalating group in higher education, have only recently begun to receive attention (Hsai and Hirano-Nakanishi, 1989). Kiang (1992), referring to U.S. Department of Education 1990 data, states that 40 percent of all Asian Americans enrolled in higher education institutions attend two-year community colleges. The community college is a stepping-stone to the four-year sector for a large number of Asian Americans, whose profiles are typical of many immigrant and refugee students attending community college. The majority have been in the United States six years or less and are more comfortable speaking in their native language than in English and thus often experience barriers associated with language problems. They also often work at least half time while enrolled full time and have strong cultural ties and family obligations in the United States or in their home countries.

Kiang's study also identifies gender as a major factor among immigrant, refugee, and first-generation students. He states that contrary to cultural and social practices in their homelands, personal and socioeconomic factors often force Asian women to enter the world of work and school in order to survive economically as a family and become competitive in the job market as wage earners. Women's roles and traditional familial and cultural expectations are undergoing changes as a result of their entry into these domains and radically altering the traditionally male-dominated roles of leadership and authority. However, very little is known about Asian women enrolled in community colleges. The dearth of studies suggest research needs to be done that includes an examination of their academic preparation, career choices, financial and child-care needs, juggling of roles within the family, employment, and cultural community.

Black Women Students. In her landmark case study of an urban community college culture, Weis (1985, 1992) clearly illuminates the race, class, and gender differences that often exist in the community college environment. She focuses on "three axes of tension: those between black and white students, those between the black middle-class faculty and the black urban poor students, and those between black male and black female students" (1992, p. 14). The gender tensions Weis describes between black males and females go beyond the classroom doors and are part of larger societal concerns. Thus they are difficult to disentangle within the educational context only. Weis found, however, that the desire to provide a better life for the family is a major reason for black females to attend community college. The research on reentry women students (Feiger, 1991) supports this finding: women's desire to improve their life situation and/or to be able to offer a better life to their children are often among the main socioeconomic reasons why many of them, regardless of their race and ethnicity, enroll in college.

Using the words of the students, Weis (1992) illustrates the different pressures black female students experience and believes that black male students do not have or do not have to the degree black females do. These pressures typically include having to balance family, work, and schooling coupled with financial concerns. As a result, making every minute count and lacking adequate time to study and prepare for classes seem to be the main problems for most black women no matter how serious they are about their roles as students. According to Feiger's findings (1991), these pressures are not unlike the pressures all women students experience.

Native American Women Students. In his description of students enrolled in tribal colleges, most of which are two-year colleges, Stein (1992) states that the majority of Native American students enrolled are female single heads of households with extended family obligations. Attending college, finding time to study and prepare for their courses, and balancing family life are difficult burdens for these students. To assist their students, some tribal colleges provide child care along with transportation services and may provide a women's support group. Cultural aspects of the American Indian culture, as described by Stein, provide a source of internal conflict for students. For example, a strong tribal value "is that of putting the interests or welfare of the family and tribe ahead of any individual's desires or needs. When a family member or close friend decides to embark on a path that will take that person out of the familiar circle of the family . . . this change is often seen as a form of desertion" (p. 95).

In sum, the research and literature on women of color is scant. We found a little more on Hispanic than on African American, Native American, and Asian women students. Nonetheless, we conclude that in light of what our search uncovered, there is still very little research being done on any of these ethnic groups. The gaps remains not only at the aggregate racial/ethnic level but at the more distinct cultural group levels as well. For example, under Hispanic women students, studies we reviewed focus on the female student of Mexican descent. Other Hispanic groups are not addressed in these works. The same limitation exists for other works discussed.

Implications for Research and Practice

The few studies about Hispanic, Native American, black, and Asian women indicate that women of color often face strong cultural obligations to their families, such as caring for family members and other in-home and out-of-home responsibilities. These obligations cannot be ignored by the women or the community college. Additional research is crucial to learning more about the factors that impede or facilitate academic progress for all groups by gender, race/ethnicity, and institutional level. Such studies must be undertaken because they will help community college policymakers and practitioners to recognize, understand, and improve conditions for all students, including women and those of color.

The studies reviewed here often describe women community college students of different socioeconomic statuses, ages, and racial/ethnic groups. They are portrayed as active, dynamic, involved, eager individuals who are trying to gain some control over their lives in areas denied to them by society at large or impeded by more personal cultural and/or financial circumstances. They question the power structures of their world, their attributed positions within the authoritarian hierarchical arrangements, and work to change their ascribed order and influence within them. As students, they are willing to assume additional stress and hardships temporarily while working energetically toward future goals and better lives than their present or past ones offer. Furthermore, they defy the myth of nontraditional students as disadvantaged, seemingly helpless victims relegated to the lower rungs of society. Instead, they offer counterimages of strength, direction, confidence, and power once they experience academic success and validation of their own worth in their local community colleges. In short, they are women like Sylvia, introduced at the beginning of this chapter, women who can achieve personal and professional success in a supportive environment and who credit the community college experience in part for helping them accomplish their goals and achieve their dreams of a better life.

Researchers and practitioners alike can use these vivid images of community college women to inform their work in new and interesting ways that also serve to promote and enhance the educational opportunities for this population that represents more than 50 percent of those attending the community college. The community college can use its institutional authority to empower its women students by offering programs that facilitate their progress and mitigate the obstacles and stresses which impede it. Special programs offering additional financial aid to cover child care, transportation, extra tutoring sessions, and understanding faculty and administrators can increase the persistence and completion rate of all women. Offering required orientation sessions for all new students; consolidating information related to majors, certificate, associate degree, and transfer programs in a central location in the college; refocusing the curriculum, activities to encourage women to explore less traditional majors and career fields; establishing transfer centers that focus on women and underrepresented racial/ethnic groups; and reaching out into the high schools and communities are just a few of the changes community colleges can and are making to facilitate women's progress.

References

Astin, A. W. *Minorities in American Higher Education.* San Francisco: Jossey-Bass, 1988.

Brint, S., and Karabel, J. *The Diverted Dream.* New York: Oxford University Press, 1989.

Carter, D. *Policy Brief.* Washington, D.C.: Office of Minority Concerns, 1992.

Carter, D., and Wilson, R. *Eleventh Annual Report on the Status of Minorities in Higher Education.* Washington, D.C.: Office of Minority Concerns, 1993. (ED 363 250)

Carter, D., and Wilson, R. *Twelfth Annual Report on the Status of Minorities in Higher Education.* Washington, D.C.: Office of Minority Concerns, 1994.

Chacon, M. A., Cohen, E. G., and Strover, S. "Chicanos and Chicanas: Barriers to Progress in Higher Education." In M. Olivas (ed.), *Latino College Students.* New York: Teachers College Press, 1986.

Cohen, A. M. "Degree Achievement by Minorities in Community Colleges." *Research in Higher Education,* 1988, *11* (4), 383–402.

Cohen, A. M., and Brawer, F. B. *The Collegiate Function of Community Colleges.* San Francisco: Jossey-Bass, 1987.

Cohen, A. M., and Brawer, F. B. *The American Community College* (2nd ed.). San Francisco: Jossey-Bass, 1989.

Cross, K. P. *Beyond the Open Door.* San Francisco: Jossey-Bass, 1971.

Eaton, J. S. "Editor's Notes." In J. S. Eaton (ed.), *Women in Community Colleges.* New Directions for Community Colleges, no. 34. San Francisco: Jossey-Bass, 1981.

Feiger, H. T. "The American Community College Woman." Unpublished doctoral dissertation, University of California, Los Angeles, 1991.

Gittell, M. "A Place for Women?" In L. S. Zwerling (ed.), *TheCommunity College and Its Critics.* New Directions for Community Colleges, no. 54. San Francisco: Jossey-Bass, 1986.

Hsai, J., and Hirano-Nakanishi, M. "The Demographics of Diversity: Asian Americans and Higher Education. *Change,* Nov./Dec. 1989, pp. 20–27.

Kiang, P. N. "Issues of Curriculum and Community for First-Generation Asian Americans in College." In L. S. Zwerling, L. London, and H. London (eds.), *First-Generation Students: Confronting the Cultural Issues.* New Directions for Community Colleges, no. 80. San Francisco: Jossey-Bass, 1992.

Laden, B. V. "The Transfer Function: Issues and Concerns." Paper presented at Community College Conference, Educational Testing Service, Princeton, N.J., June 1990.

Laden, B. V. "The Educational Pipeline: Organizational and Protective Factors Influencing Academic Progress Toward Transfer of Hispanic Community College Students with Potential at Risk Characteristics." Unpublished doctoral dissertation, Stanford University, 1994.

LaPaglia, N. *Storytellers: The Image of the Two-Year College in American Fiction and Women's Journals.* DeKalb, Ill.: LEPS Press, Northern Illinois University, 1994.

Long, H. B., and Blanchard, D. "Women Students: The Community/Junior College Connection." *Community/Junior College,* 1991, *15* (47), 47–56.

Nora, A. "Two-Year Colleges and Minority Students' Educational Aspirations: Help or Hindrance?" In J. L. Smart (ed.), *Higher Education: Handbook of Theory and Research,* Vol. 9, 1993.

Olivas, M. A. *The Dilemma of Access: Minorities in Two-Year Colleges.* Washington, D.C.: Howard University Press, 1979.

Rendon, L. "From the Barrio to the Academy: Revelations of a Mexican American Scholarship Girl." In L. S. Zwerling, L. Steven, and H. London (eds.), *First-Generation Students: Confronting the Cultural Issues.* New Directions for Community Colleges, no. 80. San Francisco: Jossey-Bass, 1992.

Richardson, R. C., Jr., and Bender, L. W. *Fostering Minority Access and Achievement in Higher Education.* San Francisco: Jossey-Bass, 1987.

Stein, W. J. "Tribal Colleges: A Success Story." In L. S. Zwerling and H. London (eds.), *First-Generation Students: Confronting the Cultural Issues.* New Directions for Community Colleges, no. 80. San Francisco: Jossey-Bass, 1992.

Turner, C. S. "The Structure of Student Communication: Living Within the Network." Paper presented at the American Educational Research Association, San Francisco, Oct. 1984. (ED 259 594)

Twombly, S. B. "What We Know About Women in Community Colleges: An Examination of the Literature Using Feminist Phase Theory." *Journal of Higher Education,* 1993, *64* (2), 186–210.

Weis, L. *Between Two Worlds: Black Students in an Urban Community College.* Boston: Routledge and Kegan Paul, 1985.

Weis, L. "Discordant Voices in the Community College." In L. S. Zwerling and H. London (eds.), *First-Generation Students: Confronting the Cultural Issues.* New Directions for Community Colleges, no. 80. San Francisco: Jossey-Bass, 1992.

BERTA VIGIL LADEN is assistant professor of higher education at Vanderbilt University.

CAROLINE SOTELLO VIERNES TURNER is associate professor in educational policy and administration at the University of Minnesota, Twin City campus.

Student services must move away from a male-oriented perspective that sees women's needs as peripheral and begin to view women's needs as central concerns of the community college.

Engendering Student Services

Mildred García

As of 1991, there were 1,469 community colleges nationally with a total of 5,651,900 students. In 1963 community college enrollments represented 17.8 percent of the higher education enrollment; by 1991 two-year college students represented almost 40 percent of the 14,358,953 students enrolled in higher education (Snyder and Hoffman, 1993).

Women students are now in the majority at community colleges, just as they are in all of higher education. Women are almost 55 percent of the total fall 1991 enrollment in colleges and universities, and over 41 percent of the fall 1991 enrollment of women students was in two-year schools. Part-time enrollment in community colleges has also increased dramatically in the last few decades, partly because of the growing enrollment of women. In the fall of 1991, 63 percent of community college students were part time; women part-time students were almost 38 percent of the community college's total enrollment. The National Center for Education Statistics projects that by 2004, women will continue to be the majority population in two-year schools and will represent 58 percent of the student body (Snyder and Hoffman, 1993).

As Laden and Turner indicate in Chapter Two, women community college students are ethnically diverse. More women of color are found in two-year schools than in four-year institutions: 963,725 as compared to 877,640 in the fall of 1991 (Snyder and Hoffman, 1993). As hooks (1987) notes, we cannot think of women as a single category of needs, interests, and abilities. Rather, we need to examine the higher education female population as multiple categories of learners that bring to our campuses diversity among our women and need diverse student services.

I know firsthand how community colleges can provide services conducive to the success of women of color. My entry into academia occurred at a community college. As a first generation student in 1969, I represented part of the new generation of students of color. As a first generation student from a poor working-class family, Puertoriqueña, I strove to be successful in a world that was different from my upbringing. At that time student services was the link that helped me toward completion and continuation. The peer advising services, financial aid, tutoring, and the extracurricular activities that linked my culture to education were what sparked my interest and passion. Those services were what made me decide not only to continue in education but also to work in higher education. Working at a community college became a dream for me.

LaGuardia Community College in New York, where I became a faculty member, provided me with my entry. I then began my administrative career at Hostos Community College, New York, where I was assistant to the president and the chief student affairs officer. My goal then, as it is now, was to help students of color and all disenfranchised students obtain a higher education. My parents always told us, "The best bequest that a poor family can leave their children is their education." I felt I had accomplished that goal myself and wanted to communicate that idea to the students who entered the institutions for which I worked.

One of the questions we struggled with at Hostos in the Division of Student Affairs was, "What are the specific student services needs of today's women students?" We sought to find the answers by surveys and interviews of our students. One student there told me,

> I'm the first in my family to go to college. The community college was in walking distance from home. At the age of 27, I'm a single parent and I wanted to obtain a decent paying job in order to support my child. I attend part time because I drop off Yolanda at school and take classes that end by 2 P.M. in order to pick her up at 3.

These words, echoed by many of the students who are currently enrolled in two-year schools today, were similar to ones I heard when I was a student.

How have community college student affairs professionals managed diversity and the increase of women on these campuses? What are the specific student service needs of today's women students? This chapter reviews the literature to see if these needs have been addressed, presents a feminist view of students affairs, and concludes with recommendations for practice.

Overview of Student Affairs

Given that references to student services can be traced in the literature to as early as 1924, it is surprising that literature on students services for two-year college students is so sparse. Creamer (1994), in his review of literature in this area, states that the research is based mostly on descriptive and analytic essays and occasional survey research reports.

Initially student services in the two-year college emphasized vocational guidance and orientation. During the late 1930s Cowley (1936) and Humphreys (1937) expanded the role of student services in community colleges. They saw it as one that encompasses all activities outside of the classroom and helps shape the personal development of students. By 1937 the functional roles of the student services division began to evolve. These included admissions, orientation, counseling, health, financial aid, placement, student activities, housing and personnel records, research, and services. These areas continued through the 1950s as additional services were needed. As Matson and Deegan (1985) state, these services were based on the concept of in loco parentis with student affairs professionals taking on the role of parents and authority figures.

The 1960s saw the civil rights movement, the women's movement, and the thrust by the American public for social justice. The cries for equality and open access rocked our institutions as student protesters demanded change. In response to the tenor of the times, community colleges opened their doors to a more diverse student body. Women, people of color, students of all ages, full-time students, and part-time students entered these colleges with hopes for advancement. Student affairs professionals, challenged by this phenomenon, sought to restructure and reshape their responsibilities. Presidents wanted the role of student affairs to include the calming of student takeovers and rebellions. Professionals and national organizations directed their energies in shaping student affairs to encompass a comprehensive array of services. Indeed, the most comprehensive list of the student affairs role was presented in the mid 1960s and was influenced by a committee of the American Association of Junior Colleges. The committee presented to the colleges its vision for student affairs and divided student affairs' responsibilities into seven functions: orientation, appraisal, participation, consultation, regulation, service, and organization (Collins, 1967).

Not surprisingly, throughout the documented history of student affairs, the profession is chronicled as either one that segregated services to women and men by having deans of women and men or one that treated the services as gender neutral. Although women were enrolling in large numbers and included not only traditional age women but also returning adult women and ethnically diverse women, their presence was not really acknowledged. Not until the 1970s was there an emergence of programs that began to address the women studying within these institutions. Programs emerged that were designed to accommodate and assist this new population. Women's centers were established, counseling services for women were instituted, and women's studies programs were added to the curriculum.

By the 1980s the enrollment of women continued to rise rapidly. The percentage of women enrolled in community colleges in the 1980s reached 20 percent of the total college population and 55 percent of the community college population. However, higher education began to experience the continuing fiscal crises we are still struggling with today. Even with these budgetary constraints, institutions recognized the necessity of instituting and reinforcing services to address the needs of this ever-increasing population. Women became more vocal and communicated their needs to the administration. Administrators recognized, sometimes for moral reasons and sometimes for economic ones, that women students were vital to institutional survival. Concern for women-centered programs grew in momentum and throughout the decade day-care centers sprang up on campuses and family planning counseling was initiated. There was also a continuance of programs established in the previous decade, such as career counseling for women, consciousness raising groups, reentry programs for women, and women's centers.

Structural Power and Student Affairs

In the 1990s feminist perspectives on society, family, and individual women have shaped thinking within academic circles. However, community college leaders do not seem to have considered or acknowledged the power relations and power imbalances between men and women. Nor have they considered feminist perspectives in revisiting and revising the roles and functions of student affairs. The division of student affairs is part and parcel of a male-centered and dominated organizational structure. The division itself has been structured in such a way as to silence the definition of the role of women and obscure and devalue the history of women. Through this male-dominated structure, women's voices have been disregarded.

The male paradigm and male presence was the standard on which the profession was established. This male standard denied women a normal presence in the structural formation of student affairs. Because of this historical foundation, services created in the 1970s and 1980s to assist women students were seen as add-on activities, ones that sit at the periphery of the organization. This point is illustrated by Elsner and Ames's (1983) attempt to rethink student affairs. They suggest the following three categories for student services in community colleges: "(1) institutionally based services—those services that are essential to the function of the college, such as admissions; (2) situationally based services—those that may be required because of special circumstances, such as child care; and (3) special interest or developmental services—which provide assistance to special groups, such as support services for re-entering women" (p. 139). In other words, support services for women and child care are not "essential to the function of the college" (Elsner and Ames, 1983, p. 139).

The assumption made in these suggestions vividly illustrates Calas and Smirich's theory (1992) that in traditional systems there is this implicit formula: "gender sex = women = problem" (p. 99). This perspective is prevalent at a time when women students are in the majority in higher education, including at community colleges. In spite of the large number of women students, their needs, such as child care, are seen as special services rather than basic ones to be offered to all students. Reentry women are seen as a special interest group. Services for these women and, indeed, for all women are seen as outside the traditional student services structure.

This attitude illustrates and reinforces how student services have been predicated on male needs and male power. Women's needs and services are added on to the male norm and thus seen as less essential. To balance the budget during times of fiscal constraints, the answer for many is to bring the organization back to the norm of male centeredness and eliminate those services viewed as unnecessary for this norm. The late 1980s and 1990s have seen a reorganization in institutions that has affected student services disproportionately. Within higher education, student services has not been viewed as an integral division; the community college is no exception to this perspective. Many of the programs within the student affairs division have been assigned to the chief academic office. Those services that have given support to women, services such as women's centers, child care, and health and wellness programs, either have had their funding reduced or have been eliminated. Services helpful to women and other disenfranchised people are frequently seen by those in power as wasteful and expendable.

How do student services take into account the social and cultural as well as educational needs of women? To what extent are student services responsive to the lives, experiences, and needs of African American, Asian, Latina, and Native American women? To what extent are student services responsive to poor, lesbian, or disabled women? These are questions that student affairs professionals need to examine as we look toward the year 2000.

How a Feminist Approach Can Change Student Affairs Today

Feminism as a movement realizes a genuine power imbalance between men and women, with the power imbalance working to favor men. Feminist goals include equality, liberation, and integrity. I believe the community college can become a feminist organization. Because it has a critical mass of women students, it can be the springboard to prepare both women and men for a new world in which power relations are more equal between them. Providing a liberating education would allow students to learn without being blocked by gender discrimination and would facilitate students' attainment of skills and credentials necessary for career success and fulfilling lives. In such a system, the subordinate position of women as students would be erased.

How can these theories of empowerment influence the practice of student services in community colleges? First and foremost, the feminist movement needs to learn from its errors. Oppressed women are not only those of white middle-class backgrounds. The community college, as a microcosm of a diverse society, illustrates that women come from all walks of life. Furthermore, the services currently offered need to be critically analyzed and challenged to determine whether the traditional manner with which these services have been offered is appropriate for women of all colors and from all socioeconomic classes, as well as for diverse groups of men. These services need to be offered in ways that validate the experiences, languages, and cultures the students bring and allow students to mesh their experiences into the web of knowledge. Students need an environment in which they can accept themselves while joining the academic enterprise. The needs that students bring and the voices they contribute must be seen as valid contributions to the community college enterprise.

It is important to note that in a feminist organization, child care would be seen as an essential priority for providing both men and women with educational equity and empowerment. The absence of or limited offering of childcare services in many of our community colleges underscores the patriarchical society that restricts women's empowerment through education. In short, student services needs to embrace the circumstances students bring with them and to see the assistance offered as essential to the mission of student affairs professions and the institution.

Recommendations for Practice and Research

What can community college student affairs personnel do to address issues of gender and power in the community college? Working at institutions that provide access to higher education, student service professionals can play the role of architects for building change rather than gatekeepers to maintain the current inequitable structure. Maximizing student potential requires monitoring what community college student services offer and what the current student population brings with it and the needs it has. In that light I make the following recommendations:

1. Validating women students as knowers is essential to providing responsive student services. For example, has the institution conducted a needs assessment of women students in particular as well as students in general? Have student affairs committees included women students? Recognizing the necessity of bringing women into full partnership in the recreation of student affairs will increase the possibility of engendering student affairs.

2. Services generally need to allow for women's needs as they partake of education. Although most students have responsibilities in addition to their education, women students tend to have primary responsibility for child care, elder care, and home care or housework. Student service professionals need to examine the scheduling of office hours, extracurricular activities, and counseling—in essence, all student services—to address the reality of women's (and men's) lives in today's society.

An excellent example of an institutional response to the reality of the lives of their students is Kingsborough Community College's establishment of its Family College. One of the first to implement a program that addresses the needs of parents and their many responsibilities, Kingsborough developed Family College as a program for women receiving social service benefits. While the mothers attend classes on campus, so do their children. Education is seen as a family event and joint graduations are held.

3. Connecting institution to community can sensitize student affairs in areas where they cannot afford to expand. As fiscal constraints become an ever-growing reality for most colleges, institutions need to look to the multitude of community services as resources for students. At Hostos Community College a multiservices center was created in 1983. Directed by one of the counselors in student affairs, the center was to identify and connect with the myriad services offered in the area. When a student communicated a need for which there were no services at Hostos, the center found the community agency that best satisfied this need and connected the agency and the student. Hospitals, social service agencies, support groups, psychiatric services, housing referrals, elder care, family planning—all became part of the extended student services division. Through this type of service the students' individual needs were addressed and barriers that inhibited successful participation of students in their educational enterprise were eliminated.

4. As a collaborative community, students and professionals need to learn how to learn and live within a diverse society. Once the diversity within the institution has been recognized, diversity in the fullest meaning of its term must be incorporated. Although an institution may be represented by only certain groups, the possibility that students will encounter other groups upon leaving the institution is a reality. The responsibility of those in the institution is to prepare students to be successful with people of both genders and all races and classes.

Too often institutions lose opportunities to hire role models who will bring diversity of thought and perspective. A search for a dean of students at a predominantly white institution brought forward two finalists: one majority woman and one woman of color. Both were competent, qualified women who were ready for a career move. The appointing authority stated that this was the hardest personnel decision he had ever made. The majority woman was hired. The appointing authority stated that the woman of color was eliminated because the student government representatives had concerns. There were five students involved in the search, all majority students. This incident occurred in a state that has one of the most segregated school systems in the country. It is true that student voices must be heard, but it must be all student voices. Where were the representatives of the organizations that represent the diversity that has begun on this campus? How will students learn to work with all people if only one type of person is continually hired?

5. Career counselors need to be alert to how many students, regardless of their race, class, or gender, bring with them oppressive mind-sets. There is a critical need to reveal the wealth of opportunities and options available to students. In this way students can avoid career choices that track them into stereotypical roles, such as women opting for secretarial work and men opting for electrical engineering.

6. Every level of the institution should strive to employ women and men with a feminist perspective. These people will be sensitive to the diverse student body and will not embrace the male-dominated status quo. The type of individuals needed in student affairs today are professionals who are themselves feminists, multicultural in thought, and supportive of both women and men who are beginning their educational journey. Together professionals and students will create environments that are responsive to the students who come into the institution.

7. The dearth of information about women and student services in community colleges is alarming. Furthermore, the impact of feminist thought on community colleges and the possible transformation of these institutions is not addressed in the literature. Research that addresses the reshaping and/or reconstructing of student services is vitally needed. Examination of new structures for change by professionals, researchers, and students would push for ways of transforming the student services profession.

In collaboration with what occurs in community college classrooms, student services is a vital agent for change with the constituency it serves. As the most diverse institution of higher education, the community college can become a model in demonstrating how to create a collaborative, risk-free environment that maximizes the potential of its students. This kind of transformation cannot take place without the involvement of student affairs professionals. Change of this magnitude can only occur, however, when true access and retention are examined in their fullest meaning, and organizational structures, policies, and practices are transformed. Through this examination and transformation, women and men of all colors, races, and socioeconomic classes can thrive, study in full partnership with each other, and leave community colleges to lead responsible and fulfilling lives with their families and communities. As change agent professionals, student service personnel have the power to initiate and forge the process that will enable the success of all the students they serve.

References

Calas, M. B., and Smirich, L. "Re-writing Gender into Organizational Theorizing: Direction from Feminist Perspectives." In J. S. Glazer, E. M. Bensimon, and B. K. Townsend (eds.), *Women in Higher Education: A Feminist Perspective*. Boston: Ginn, 1993.

Collins, C.C. *Junior College Student Personnel Programs: What They Are and What They Should Be*. Washington, D.C.: American Association of Junior Colleges, 1967.

Cowley, W. H. "The Nature of Personnel Work." *Educational Record*, 1936, 42, 218.

Creamer, D. G. "Synthesis of Literature Related to Historical and Current Functions of Student Services." In G. A. Baker, III (ed.), *A Handbook on the Community College in America*. Westport, Conn.: Greenwood Press, 1994.

Elsner, P., and Ames, W. C. "Redirecting Student Services." In G. B. Vaughan and Associates, *Issues for Community College Leaders in a New Era*. San Francisco: Jossey-Bass, 1983.

hooks, b. *Talking Back*. Boston: South End Press, 1989.

Humphreys, J. A. "Personnel Service in the Junior College." *Junior College Journal*, 1937, 52, 382–392.

Matson, J. E., and Deegan, W. L. "Revitalizing Student Services." In W. L. Deegan, D. Tillery, and Associates, *Renewing the American Community College.* San Francisco: Jossey-Bass, 1985.
Snyder, T. D., and Hoffman, C. M. *Digest of Education Statistics 1993.* Washington, D.C.: Office of Educational Research and Improvement, U.S. Department of Education, Oct. 1993.

MILDRED GARCÍA is assistant vice president for academic affairs at Montclair State University, New Jersey.

Because women community college faculty are understudied, we do not know how they perceive their position within the institution.

Women Community College Faculty: On the Margins or in the Mainstream?

Barbara K. Townsend

If numbers signify power, then women faculty are an important force in the community college. In 1991–92, almost 45 percent of full-time faculty in colleges offering the A.A. degree were women: 43.2 percent in the public sector and 54.1 percent in the private. By comparison, in four-year schools offering the B.A., only 35 percent of the full-time faculty were women; in doctoral-granting institutions barely 26 percent were women (Touchton and Davis, 1991, p. 28).

Comprising almost half the institution's full-time faculty, women faculty would seem to be in the mainstream in community colleges. However, those who study the professoriate view the high numbers of women community college faculty as evidence of the marginalization of women as faculty (Finkelstein, 1984; Moore and Sagaria, 1991). Implicit in this perspective is the view that the community college is a marginal institution, operating outside the mainstream of higher education. Those who teach in it are second-class citizens in the academic world. From this perspective, women two-year college faculty are marginalized at the margins: as women they are automatically marginalized and as faculty, they are marginalized by working in the community college.

How accurate a picture is this? Are women faculty in the two-year college marginal citizens in academe? Additionally, within the two-year college, are women faculty operating in the institutional mainstream or at its margins? To answer these questions, I discuss why there are so many women full-time faculty in two-year colleges, what we know and do not know about them, and conclude with suggestions for future research and practice.

Why So Many Women Faculty in Two-Year Colleges?

Although the percentage of women faculty in all of higher education has increased in the last thirty years, much of the increase can be attributed to the growth of the two-year sector. Why are there more women faculty in the community college than in any other type of higher education institution? Is it because community college leaders have consciously striven to hire women, or is their strong numerical presence attributable to other causes?

Baldridge, Curtis, Ecker, and Riley (1978) indicate that the "over-representation of women faculty in two-year colleges" is partially the result of the tremendous growth of this institution in the twentieth century, from 207 schools in 1920 to 694 in 1969 (p. 180). So many faculty had to be hired that even women were able to get faculty positions. The implication is that women owe their presence in the two-year college to sector expansion, not to any commitment on the part of community colleges to hire women.

Similarly, Dziech (1983) notes with the expansion of higher education in the 1960s, four-year institutions had first choice of available faculty and usually hired males. Community college administrators had to turn to secondary schools to find faculty, with the result that many women faculty were hired. However, "there was little concern for sexual balance or equity" (p. 57). Women community college faculty were not hired for altruistic or ideological reasons but for pragmatic ones.

In sum, the hiring of women faculty in community colleges resulted from the need to hire faculty, period. Because there were not always enough men available to be hired, women were hired. Hiring women was a necessity, not a desire.

What Do We Know About the Lives of Women Community College Faculty?

No matter why they were hired, there are a lot of women faculty in the community college. Given their large numbers, one might expect to find them a highly researched group. However, women community college faculty are almost unstudied (Twombly, 1993). For example, an ERIC search for references on women faculty in the two-year or community college yielded 29 references for the years 1966 to 1981 and 30 references for the years 1982 to 1992. When these references were examined, almost all were to studies in which gender or sex was used as a variable in a study.

One reason for the lack of attention to women community college faculty is that community college faculty in general are not often studied. Because research is not required as part of their professional responsibilities, they have less motivation than university professors to do "navel gazing." Also, some university professors may not conduct research on community colleges because the professors perceive, perhaps erroneously, that this research is deemed less acceptable and less prestigious than research on four-year colleges and universities. When I began my career as a university professor of higher education, my department chair told me, "We're not interested in research on that topic [community colleges] here."

An occasional scholar, often from the community college sector, does study women who teach at two-year colleges. In the 1970s a few researchers provided snapshots of these women and their beliefs. In a brief report on 1972 survey data about women faculty in 17 two-year schools in Maryland, Weekly (1974) notes that 25 percent of the 220 respondents indicated women were discriminated against in these institutions. Some believed the discrimination occurred when women sought faculty and administrative positions, and some believed women students experienced discrimination in such areas as career counseling and financial aid. Drawing from a 1975 national survey, Brawer (1977) developed a profile of male and female faculty (full and part time) who taught the humanities. She concludes, "Differences between women and men—while present—are not marked, suggesting that people are people—their differences are not attributable as much to sex as to individual differences among people in general" (p. 22).

In the 1980s Hankin (1984), a community college president, conducted two studies to ascertain the number of women and minorities faculty and administrators in public two-year schools during 1983–84. Eaton's (1981) volume *Women in Community Colleges* contains two chapters on women faculty. One focuses on them almost indirectly, because the chapter is more about the humanities than about women faculty. The author urges women faculty to 'strengthen the humanities' by valu[ing], affirm[ing], and liv[ing] out" what the author labeled "feminine aspects of humanism" (Averill, 1981, p. 30). The other chapter (Price, 1981) maintains that women faculty in the two-year college do not have equal status with men faculty for a number of reasons, most of which pertain to all women, not just faculty.

Seidman's (1985) study of two-year faculty, both male and female, provides important understandings of their professional lives. From his interviews with 76 faculty in three states (Massachusetts, California, and New York), Seidman found that women faculty were troubled by sexist attitudes, which seemed to work against their ability to obtain and succeed in administrative positions.

Different concerns are evidenced in LaPaglia's (1994) look at women faculty. In an effort to learn more about community college students, she asked 14 women faculty from five two-year schools in three states to keep an open-ended journal of their observations about students and the community college. Although the focus of her research is students rather than faculty, what emerges in the journals is the faculty's awareness that the culture has ascribed a "marginal status" (p. 116) to community college students and faculty alike.

Because the research on women faculty in the community college is so limited, I draw on my own experience as a full-time community college faculty member as well as on the research to sketch a portrait of the professional lives of these women.

Professional Status. I taught developmental English and study skills at a two-year school in Virginia for eight years (1976–1984). I remember my pride in becoming a community college faculty member for I had obtained a higher status teaching job than the secondary education one for which I had prepared as an undergraduate. Also, I felt very fortunate as a mother because my teaching schedule permitted me to be home when my son arrived from school.

For many women faculty, teaching full time in a two-year college is the ideal employment. Given that faculty members have some flexibility in scheduling their work hours, women faculty are better able to combine having a career with raising families than are K–12 teachers, let alone people who work in business and industry. Teaching in the two-year college also provides more status than teaching in K–12 education, which at least in the 1960s and 1970s was the major career opportunity for many women. As Seidman (1985) notes, "particularly [for] women, the community college represents a level of achievement they had not even considered possible for themselves" (p. 11).

Although I was proud of being a two-year college faculty member, I felt the disdain of faculty from four-year institutions. At professional conferences, colleagues would almost visibly shrink back once they learned where I taught. It was not because I was a woman that I experienced this negative reaction. It was because I was a community college faculty member. Both male and female two-year faculty are often seen by four-year faculty as marginal members of academe.

The reasons for this are several. First of all, two-year college faculty generally lack the educational credentials to be hired in the four-year sector. Although almost 70 percent of faculty at public comprehensive colleges and 90 percent at public research universities hold the Ph.D., less than 20 percent of full-time community college faculty do so (Russell and others, 1990). Two-year faculty also have work roles that can be viewed as somewhat marginal or undesirable in academe. Their primary responsibility is to transmit knowledge rather than to advance it through research. They must teach and teach often. Working in open-door institutions, they must also teach many students who would not be admitted to four-year schools. As egalitarian as Americans claim to be, status still resides with faculty who teach the best and the brightest, not the average and the slow. Also, with a typical course load of four to five courses a semester, two-year faculty have little time to conduct research, even if they want to. Encouragement of classroom research, in which faculty research how well their students are learning in a particular course, is common in the two-year sector now, but such research is usually considered too practitioner oriented to be esteemed in the four-year sector.

Discriminatory Practices. Although four-year faculty experience greater professional status within the academy than do two-year faculty, two-year women faculty may benefit from an institutional environment that is more receptive to them as women. I believe I have encountered more discrimination in the form of sexist behavior in the university setting than in the community

WOMEN COMMUNITY COLLEGE FACULTY   43

college. Although it may be that over the years I have simply developed better radar for detecting sexism, another explanation is that the environment of the community college is less conducive to sexism than is the university.

National evidence corroborating this perspective may be found in faculty responses to the national 1989–90 Higher Education Research Institution (HERI) Faculty Survey. When faculty were asked sources of stress, almost 50 percent of all female respondents indicated "subtle discrimination" as a source of stress. However, almost 52 percent of all four-year faculty identified it as compared to about 39 percent of two-year faculty (Astin, Korn, and Dey, 1991).

Regardless of what institutional setting they are in, women experience sexist attitudes because these attitudes are part of the sociocultural environment in which higher education institutions operate. However, the high numbers of women faculty and administrators in the community college may help mitigate sexist attitudes. Women faculty aspiring to administrative positions as department chair or division head do not lack for role models because these positions are frequently held by women. Similarly, women teaching in a two-year school are more likely to have a female president than are women in four-year colleges and universities.

Another reason why there may be less sexism in the two-year college is because there are fewer opportunities for status differentials between men and women than in four-year schools. Tenure is much more easily attained in the two-year college than in the four-year institution. Usually, a community college instructor receives tenure after three consecutive years of full-time teaching. Also, many community colleges do not have the hierarchy of professorial ranks. Even when there are academic ranks, promotion to associate or full professor is primarily based on years of service and possession of a doctorate. Movement up the professorial hierarchy is thus less subject to power imbalances resulting from gender discrimination.

This is not to say that sexism does not exist in the community college. In Seidman's (1985) study of community college faculty, several of the women spoke about the sexism they encountered. Summarizing their concerns, Seidman notes, "women confront sexist attitudes about their salary and status and must contend with double standards, both in work and social situations in the college. They find they must constantly cater to or figure out a way to go around traditional male assumptions about who has good ideas and how best to get things done" (pp. 268–269). One manifestation of sexism is sexual harassment. As Riggs and Murrell indicate in Chapter Six, we know little about sexual harassment in the community college. Given that "the ratio of males to females can facilitate or inhibit sexual harassment" (Tangri, Burt, and Johnson, 1982, p. 38), it may be less prevalent in the community college because the ratio of male to female faculty is about equal.

Another manifestation of sexism or unequal treatment is lower salaries and lower ranks for women faculty. Lack of institutional commitment to equity is suggested in the results of Singh's (1991) study of trends in salaries and ranks of women faculty in Pennsylvania's higher education institutions from 1971 to 1989. She found that women were more apt to be employed in community colleges than in any other institutional type. However, women community college faculty endured salary inequity regardless of academic rank. The same was true of women faculty in all other institutional types.

Hiring women as part-time rather than as full-time instructors is another way to marginalize them. The majority of part-time instructors in the community college are women (Cohen and Brawer, 1992). As Albert and Watson (1980) note, "the high proportion of women in this group [of community college part-timers] could be considered an example of the discriminatory treatment of women in academe" (p. 93).

Implications for Research and Practice

Public conversation, as manifested in the rhetoric of community college spokespersons or in the discourse of academic journals, presents a dualistic perspective on community college women faculty. Their presence is viewed either as the result of enlightened leadership aiming to practice inclusion in hiring and admission practices (Gillett-Karam, Roueche, and Roueche, 1990–91) or as one more example of the continued oppression and marginalization of women faculty through their regulation to an inferior academic institution (Dzech, 1983; Finkelstein, 1984).

The primary existing evidence for the argument that community colleges affect women negatively is Seidman's study (1985), which is now a decade old, and LaPaglia's (1994), which is rather limited in scope. However, LaPaglia's comments do cast some light on one of the questions that frames this chapter: Are women faculty marginal in the community college? She reports, "Every faculty journal discusses the marginality of their students, both as it is experienced by the students and as it is perceived by the larger culture. In addition, about half of them write about their own assigned marginality as two-year college teachers. Inside the system they are all business; outside they are aware of their low status" (p. 121). What LaPaglia's research suggests is that community college faculty, women and men, perceive they are regarded as marginal in academe and in the larger society because the two-year college is regarded as a marginal institution. Although national and institutional leaders of the two-year college tout its importance to postsecondary education and to the nation, this importance is apparently not always understood or believed by constituencies in four-year schools. Similarly, society in general values the community college to a certain extent, but still may perceive it as "less than" four-year institutions and view its students and faculty as marginal in relation to four-year colleges and universities. Thus LaPaglia's research suggests a "yes" answer to the question, Do women community college faculty perceive themselves as university researchers do—as being on the margins of higher education because they are in the community college?

What is less clear is whether community college women faculty perceive themselves to be marginal *within* the institution as compared to male faculty. More broadly, do women two-year faculty members see and feel what male two-year faculty do? Do women and men faculty members share a common vision of the community college, its students, curriculum, and administrative practices? Or does the vision of women faculty differ because they perceive themselves to be outsiders, living on the margins of a patriarchal institution?

Many university women faculty do perceive themselves in this way. The problem of their marginality is being addressed in some innovative institutions by development of a mentoring program to assist junior faculty in attaining tenure (Wunsch, 1994). Do women two-year faculty have the same need for mentoring that four-year women faculty do? Or does the relative ease with which tenure is obtained in the two-year school mitigate against the need for mentoring? Would mentoring assist women faculty to achieve more positions of power in the two-year school through such activities as teaching them what faculty committees are important and how they could become department chair or division head?

Also, the power of unions in the two-year college and their possible effect on gender relations needs to be examined. Unlike four-year institutions, many two-year colleges are unionized. Union leaders may well be more powerful in the two-year school than department heads and faculty senates. How many union leaders are women, and how receptive to women as leaders are community college unions? Does the existence of labor unions affect gender relations in the two-year college and if so, how? (personal correspondence, Nancy LaPaglia, June 10, 1994).

We need to research these and other questions to learn how two-year college women faculty, both full and part time, understand their experiences. A note of caution is needed here: gender is but one lens through which to view the experiences of community college faculty. We also need to differentiate their experiences in terms of race/ethnicity, age, social class, physical condition, marital status, and sexual orientation. There is a multiplicity of experiences that has yet to be tapped by those who wish to understand faculty in the community college and develop institutional practices that effectively utilize their strengths and abilities.

References

Albert, L. S., and Watson, R. J. "Mainstreaming Part-Time Faculty: Issue or Imperative?" In M. H. Parsons (ed.), *Using Part-Time Faculty Effectively.* New Directions for Community Colleges, no. 30. San Francisco: Jossey-Bass, 1980.
Astin, A. W., Korn, W. S., and Dey, E. L. *The American College Teacher: National Norms for the 1989–90 HERI Faculty Survey.* Los Angeles: Higher Education Research Institute, University of California, Mar. 1991.
Averill, L. "How Can Women Influence Humanities Education?" In J. S. Eaton (ed.), *Women in Community Colleges.* New Directions for Community Colleges, no. 34. San Francisco: Jossey-Bass, 1981.

Baldridge, J. V., Curtis, D., Ecker, G., and Riley, G. L. *Policy Making and Effective Leadership.* San Francisco: Jossey-Bass, 1978.

Brawer, F. "Women in Community Colleges: A Profile." *Community College Frontiers,* 1977, 5 (3), 19–22.

Cohen, A., and Brawer, F. *The American Community College.* San Francisco: Jossey-Bass, 1992.

Dziech, B. W. "Changing Status of Women." In G. Vaughan (ed.), *Issues for Community College Leaders in a New Era.* San Francisco: Jossey-Bass, 1983.

Eaton, J. S. "Editor's Notes." In J. S. Eaton (ed.), *Women in Community Colleges.* New Directions for Community Colleges, no. 34. San Francisco: Jossey-Bass, 1981.

Finkelstein, M. J. *The American Academic Profession.* Columbus: Ohio State University Press, 1984.

Gillett-Karam, R., Roueche, S. D., and Roueche, J. E. "Under-Representation and the Question of Diversity. *Community Junior College Journal,* Dec./Jan. 1990–91, pp. 22–25.

Hankin, J. N. "Where the (Affirmative) Action Is: The Status of Minorities and Women Among the Faculty and Administrators of Public Two-Year Colleges, 1983–1984." *Journal of the College and University Personnel Association,* 1984, 35 (4), 36–39.

LaPaglia, N. *Storytellers: The Image of the Two-Year College in American Fiction and in Women's Journals.* DeKalb, Ill.: LEPS Press, Northern Illinois University, 1994.

Moore, K. M., and Sagaria, M.A.D. "The Situation of Women in Research Universities in the United States: Within the Inner Circles of Academic Power." In G. P. Kelly and S. Slaughter (eds.), *Women's Higher Education in Comparative Perspective.* Norwell, Mass.: Kluwer Academic, 1991.

Price, A. R. "Women of the Faculty." In J. Eaton (ed.), *Women in Community Colleges.* New Directions for Community Colleges, no. 34. San Francisco: Jossey-Bass, 1981.

Russell, S., Cox, R. S., Williamson, C., Boismier, J., Javitz, H., and Fairweather, J. *Faculty in Higher Education Institutions, 1988.* NCES-90-365. Washington, D.C.: National Center for Education Statistics, U.S. Department of Education, 1990.

Seidman, E. *In the Words of the Faculty.* San Francisco: Jossey- Bass, 1985.

Singh, M. K. *Trends in the Ranks and Salaries of Academic Women in Pennsylvania, 1971–1989.* Unpublished doctoral dissertation, University of Pittsburgh, 1991.

Tangri, S. S., Burt, M. R., and Johnson, L. B. "Sexual Harassment at Work: Three Explanatory Models." *Journal of Social Issues,* 1982, 38 (4), 33–54.

Touchton, J. G., and Davis, L. *Fact Book on Women in Higher Education.* New York: American Council on Education/Macmillan, 1991.

Twombly, S. "What We Know About Women in Community Colleges." *Journal of Higher Education,* 1993, 64 (2), 186–210.

Weekly, G. "The Status of Women in Maryland Community Colleges. *Community College Social Science Quarterly,* 1974, 5 (1), 23.

Wunsch, M. A. "Giving Structure to Experience: Mentoring Strategies for Women Faculty." *Initiatives,* 1994, 56 (1), 1–10.

BARBARA K. TOWNSEND is professor of higher education and chair of the Department of Leadership at the University of Memphis. For eight years she was a full-time faculty member, teaching developmental English and study skills, at Thomas Nelson Community College.

*The societal perception that both women and the working class are in
the majority in the two-year college is a major determinant of the
institution's low status and lack of visibility.*

The Interplay of Gender and Social
Class in the Community College

Nancy LaPaglia

"As virtually any feminist academic knows, one occupational hazard of doing
scholarly research on women is the possibility of failing to be taken seriously"
(Noble, 1994, p. F7). Make that research on working-class women or anyone
at a community college, and it is probable that few people will pay any attention to the work at all. A community college label is such a negative filter that
in research reports it is sometimes deleted when the authors want to be taken
seriously as writing about people who matter (Macaulay and Gonzalez, 1993;
Steinem, 1992).

Two-year college inhabitants, many of whom are women and working
class, are not only maligned or ignored in academic research but also in American culture in general. *Storytellers: The Image of the Two-Year College in American Fiction and in Women's Journals* (LaPaglia, 1994), a study I conducted of
fictional presentations of the two-year school, shows clearly how negatively it
is portrayed in the United States, including in the media of television and film.
In this chapter I first describe how the two-year college, including its students
and faculty, is portrayed in fiction as compared to the four-year school. Because
I knew from my own experience as a community college faculty member that
there is another side to the two-year college than the one seen in fiction, I
asked actual women living in the stereotypical student's and faculty's situation
to keep journals for my use. Comments from these journals are used to illustrate how different women community college students and faculty are from
the image projected by their fictional counterparts.

The Demeaning Image of the "Twos" Versus the Satirical Image of the "Fours"

"Going to college" or "graduating from the university" has never been a low-status marker in American culture. When going to college is treated in fiction, the image is not an indication of the low intelligence or ability of all who are involved in higher education. College is a step up, or at least not a step in the wrong direction. It is certainly not an action one might be embarrassed to have made public or to put on one's vita or to display on a car window decal. There is even a certain vanity in being depicted as the most animal-like of students or bumbling of professors, as long as the faculty or students are in four-year colleges, especially prestigious ones. This is true no matter how mocking the image of the college or university that is depicted.

Indeed, fiction about the "fours" is often comic in tone. Much of the humor centers around pretentious or idiosyncratic faculty misteaching thoughtless students. The college in question is usually Ivy League because more than three-quarters of college novels are set at either Harvard or Yale (Kramer, 1981; Lyons, 1962). The entertainment for the reader or viewer is often connected to a kind of envy of those who are detached from the "real" world, without the responsibility and accountability that others must bear.

Because American fiction, including the popular culture of television and film, routinely depicts four-year colleges and universities in a satirical or mocking way, how are two-year colleges treated differently? The answer to this question shows that class bias and sexism provide the key to the discrepancy between the fictional portrayals of the two-year and the four-year schools.

Whereas applications to Dartmouth, the Ivy League college that provided its setting, increased after the film *National Lampoon's Animal House* (1978), it is quite unlikely that people for whom the only option is the community college would be encouraged to enroll by the fictional images of their schools. For most writers of fiction, to put "community" and "college" together is to create an oxymoron. As Laurie Moore's central character in *Anagrams* (1986) tells us, "You might one day wake up and find yourself teaching at a community college; there will have been nothing to warn you. You might say things to your students like, There is only one valid theme in literature: Life will disappoint you."

"Community college" and "junior college" are low-status markers or shorthand for "Don't take this person or institution seriously." A Donald Barthelme character states, "In some parts of South America, armadillos grow to almost five feet in length and are allowed to teach at the junior-college level" (1987, p. 177). In a Walter Walker novel (1989), such schools are for "draft-dodgers, re-entry women and the very dumb" (p. 102). No fictional character is fondly nostalgic about the carefree, fun-filled days of higher education at a community college.

Society's image of the community college is that it is a place for powerless women, uneducated housewives, who are apparently one of the last groups of women it is still acceptable to demean in fiction. A community college student is typically portrayed as a reentry woman who is white, working class, and nontraditional in age. Passive and unenlightened, she is the sort of person to whom life just happens (Oates, 1969; Willeford, 1984).

Authors usually mock these students' taste as consumers—not their character, their sense of morality, or even their intelligence, but their working-class taste. They wear polyester, they may weigh more than the professional woman's ideal, they may be very conservative or religious or traditional in their ideas. They buy "incorrect" things when they shop or eat. In a novel set in Chicago, a graduate student from the University of Chicago teaches at a community college. Her students, like most fictional students, are marginal—at the edges of power, by definition. To her, the plastic Santas used as Christmas decor on nearby rooftops say it all about them (Schaeffer, 1973). Although she herself is highly neurotic and barely able to function, she is superior to her students because she has more elite taste.

Community college faculty are not immune from inferences they are low status, if not by background then by association with the two-year school. Fictional two-year teachers may have working-class or other low-status names (Bobbie Rae Dean of Lamar Tech and Jolene Snyder of Milwaukee C.C., for example), unlike faculty at higher status schools, who have WASP names (Oates, 1975). Some novels infer that to spend one's life as a two-year college faculty member is to be condemned to the abyss (Mackin, 1991). For women faculty, having to teach at a two-year school may cause them to drink too much brandy and wander solitary beaches, as did the central character in Marilyn French's *The Women's Room* (1977).

Other derogatory faculty stereotypes exist. The typical community college faculty member is a white male in the English department. He rarely thinks his job is important, or he may expend much of his energy on sexual liaisons with his students (Bryant, 1972; Keillor, 1991). Faculty who care about their students are rare. Most exceptions are women, and if they are assertive, they are punished for being "uppity." If they come from a working-class background, they may have an added handicap because they then find it doubly hard to feel at home in academe. If the faculty, female or male, are middle class, they find it easier to look down on their students, or at least patronize them even when feeling benevolent (Pelletier, 1985).

We can take the fictional image a step or two beyond ridicule and into punishment. "In life, as in fiction, women who speak out usually end up punished or dead" (Heilbrun, 1992, p. 47). Starting in the early 1970s, concurrent with the resurgence of the women's movement, fictional working-class women were punished for asserting "power" by enrolling in community colleges. They were called "runaway housewives." They aspired to rise above their stations in life—the American dream of having the ability to redefine yourself and transcend your social class. I found that many reentry women students and some two-year college women faculty were punished severely in fiction for their presumption in trying to gain some control of their lives (Constantine, 1982).

Often the punishment was loss of family members. "Her brain's all balled up over them books," says the mother of one thirty-four-year-old woman student who is desperately fighting her mother and husband for some control of her own life (Mason, 1982, p. 12). Are the reentry students and women faculty punished and belittled because they are women, because they are working class, or because they are at a two-year college? These categories may be inseparable in the minds of some writers.

Just how pervasive is this image of the community college as having low-status faculty and students, particularly women students? As part of my effort to collect examples of two-year college characters in fiction, I solicited leads through a letter in the *Chronicle of Higher Education*. As one might expect, a few of the leads I received were mistaken; that is, they referred to fictional works where the characters were connected to four-year schools. Each misdirection led me to low status and poorly informed fictional students at mediocre schools. Usually the students were reentry women. In other words, my correspondents misremembered their reading or viewing. If the work was about the ignorant lower classes or reentry women, it must take place in a community college.

I believe this misdirection makes my point clearly. Satirical depictions of higher education mock different aspects of the "fours" and the "twos." The two-year colleges are demeaned for their marginal inhabitants, so much so that when a devalued and "declassed" image of higher education appears, its audience assumes the college in question is not a four-year school.

Reentry Women Describe Their Own Experiences

It is ironic that the reentry woman, whatever her class, is demeaned, when for most two-year faculty, she is a valued addition to the classroom. She is in college to work and to learn. She frequently undergoes a significant change that rewards any of the faculty who care to see it. It is not the transformation into physical beauty that our fairy tales and advertising extol for women, but one marked by the joy of learning and accomplished in the face of adversity. It is strange that in fiction she is mocked or ignored for actions that could easily be praised.

Reentry women's efforts to take charge of their lives are illustrated in the part of my study that looked at journal entries written by women community college students. I believe "women's personal stories are, like all accounts of any group that has been marginalized, our best textbooks: the only way to make our experience central" (Steinem, 1992, p. 4). Furthermore, "I think ordinary people can define their own problems," instead of depending on problem definition done by elites from the university and elsewhere (Cunningham, 1990, p. 19). Therefore, I asked over three dozen women at five community colleges (located in Illinois, Oregon, and New York) to write journals for about three weeks about their experiences at two-year colleges.

Over two dozen students and fourteen faculty wrote the journals. The stories the students told were quite different from the image projected by their fictional counterparts. More specifically, four dominant themes emerged:

Agency, or making conscious choices about trying to take charge of their lives. From upstate New York: "When I started investigating career options, I tried to pick one that would only need a two-year degree, but I realized that would end up being just another job. Going to school would take all my determination and dedication, so I better be heading towards my dream. That dream is to teach."

Joy of learning, or experiencing delight in learning, especially learning that they were intelligent. From suburban Illinois: "It took me a year and a half of taking one course a semester to gain the confidence to take more. The more I took, the better I liked it. I discovered something else. I loved to learn."

Marginality, or being aware of an authoritarian arrangement that pushes them to the edges of power. From Chicago: "I am on a committee to get a Women's Studies Department established. Of course it will take time and planning to be recognized but we are persistent. We will overcome the silence of women."

Juggling, or trying to do too much, especially with too little money. From Oregon: "Maybe I'm spending too much time talking about finances, but I tell you, finances are on everyone's mind here. Financial aid is like a maze of tricks that only a few have a map to, and they won't say anything. But, hey, that's bureaucracy."

It was clear from the journals that the students assume responsibility for change in their lives, for having some power over their own fate and perhaps that of their families. They do not see themselves as victims and they do not whine, yet they see themselves as marginalized in society. What surprised me most was that more of them than I had expected understood that obtaining even limited power or control was not just an individual task. Rather, they knew to organize into groups, most often women's groups, but sometimes groups with another focus. As one student wrote, "It is hard to validate one's view or feelings in isolation."

Some of the students who wrote journals were middle class, but all face problems of one magnitude or another. Some are marginal due to class status, most are struggling financially, several are on public aid, five were high school dropouts earlier in life. One of the students, a former waitress in Chicago, has become an advocate for the poor and for street people—the people she knows. Another, Mexican American, needs to support her four children after her husband left them, and she does not want a factory job. An African American has two children, a full-time job, a full course load, and shows some understandable crankiness.

These students are aware that the college where they are registered, at great personal cost and effort, is demeaned by the larger culture. They say they are told, "That's the place of last resort." "It's the high school after high school." Within that college they are sometimes discredited further as women, usually by male faculty. Nevertheless, some students see their college as a haven in a heartless world, "a place where we are appreciated for our minds, regardless of sex." Almost all say that the college helped them to value themselves, wherever they started on the social scale. They describe a blossoming of mind and spirit. No writer says that the community college made her feel worse about herself.

Faculty's View of the Two-Year College

As Townsend indicates in Chapter Four, not only has almost nothing been written about community college women faculty, but even less has been written by these women about their situation. To help fill this void, I asked fourteen faculty women from the same five schools to write journals about their experiences in the two-year college system. Although these women also wrote of problems encountered and battles fought, the overriding import of their journals was a sense of mission and nurturing professionalism in a calling they value. (Their other main themes were a sense of marginality of their students and of themselves, and a concern for the problems of their students, including poor preparation for college-level work.)

They utilize what power they have to help one another or their students, as well as themselves, instead of using it to win over others. However, they perceive that the skills and strengths they must have in order to do this are not valued significantly by those in positions of greater power: higher level administrators, the board of trustees, or the universities. These faculty women assume a responsibility for change in their colleges, but they rarely receive the recognition that should come with it when they succeed. "I have learned that if I do all the work and let him [the administrator immediately above her] take the credit, everything will go smoothly." Women are likely to *share* power. This is a disadvantage in the larger culture.

No faculty journal writer denies the lack of academic preparation among her students. Rather, the faculty write about the many ways in which they try to meet this challenge. They also understand that having many poorly prepared students does not justify demeaning stereotypes or the lowering of standards. Their journals give a fuller picture that is rarely shown.

From each area of the country I studied, the faculty write about another problem in detail. Community colleges have long been used as a dumping ground for social services during a time of budget cuts. They are expected to deal with mental illness, poverty, crime, and other social problems. Thus the community colleges have a greater drain on resources of money and staff, including faculty, and are then given lower status for having "that kind" of student. Knowing this, these women are on a mission to help their students become more powerful, less marginal. "The open-door policy makes good on Emma Lazarus' words," says one. Another writes, "I keep thinking of that academic snob from the University of Chicago that has made his life's work out of misunderstanding the community college. Then I think of the long lines of students waiting to register for their courses—immigrants, old people . . . all looking so hopeful . . . accessible, financially feasible, leading to whatever they want, be it English 101 or a degree in nursing." And from a woman faculty member at an inner-city school: "When I talk to trustees, when I talk to people with money or authority who can help, I am a translator" between social classes. The powerful cannot understand the impact of trauma and poverty on the lives of her students.

In short, these women faculty are good illustrations of the following rare instance of praise from academia: "There are community colleges where thousands of able and intelligent men and women take their teaching opportunities with the greatest seriousness and give more than value received. These institutions . . . free for the most part of the snobbish pursuit of the latest academic fads that so warp their university counterparts . . . are, I believe, the hope of higher education in America" (Smith, 1990, p. 19).

Conclusion and Implications

Although Smith (1990) may view community colleges as "the hope of higher education in America" (p. 19), they are invisible in many ways in our culture. Nearly half of all undergraduates in the United States and almost half of all higher education faculty are at two-year colleges. Even greater percentages of minority students and faculty are at, or at least start at, two-year schools. Yet they are a tiny fraction of fictional characters, even in popular culture, and just as rarely appear in nonfiction.

Community colleges are deemed the least glamorous segment of higher education, and no one wants to hear about them. The elitist myth that regards the typical college student as a male attending school full time, living on campus, and experiencing the process of late adolescent development, hangs on long after cultural and enrollment patterns have changed. Fiction reflects this myth. Even writers who are themselves on two-year college faculties rarely include their own professional experiences in their stories, perhaps trying to avoid the stigma of being identified with those who are considered low status and colorless.

The absence of minorities in two-year college fiction is almost total. Besides, these Americans are more likely to identify with their racial or ethnic groups than with a particular social class. This is true of most of us, with few exceptions. We like to consider ourselves middle class, or ignore class altogether, although we are quite aware of class stratification no matter what racial or ethnic group in which we place ourselves or to which we are relegated. For example, a colleague who studied women in African American churches on the south side of Chicago reports that the presence of a gospel choir is a low-status marker, clearly understood by those who consider themselves from a better class (McNeil, 1994). So although she writes about gender relations that reflect power imbalances in our society, she shows that class imbalances are detrimental socially and politically as well.

Despite these issues of class and gender, the United States is still regarded as the place where upward mobility and the assumption of a new identity of one's choice are most possible. Immigrants come here by the millions, partly because they think they can transcend barriers of class and even gender more easily than in their own countries. Indeed, in fiction about two-year colleges in the 1930s, such schools functioned as the "People's College" for children of poor immigrants who sought upward mobility (Bellow, 1953). One book about a Chinese American woman from San Francisco pleased the State Department so much for its depiction of our society—so free and open that even a poor minority woman can rise to a position of affluence and power—that the government distributed the book widely in Asia and elsewhere (Wong, [1945]/1989). Thus a positive view of the "People's College" reached more readers beyond the United States than here. Two-year colleges still have this function today for immigrants and the poor, although other tasks the colleges are asked to perform dilute their original thrust. We need to celebrate this function and portray it positively in our popular culture.

Do I wish we were more open in our society about the class distinctions and disparagements we make? Would this bring two-year colleges out into a positive light, once we realized we "invisibilize" them because they are filled with low-status women? To me, the answer to both questions is yes. In this chapter I am not trying to stoke resentments by portraying all women, working-class people, and community college inhabitants as victims and martyrs. Rather, I believe that through listening to previously unheard groups tell their stories, we can obtain a clearer view, a more multifaceted view, of the interplay of gender and social class in the two-year college system, a view that can challenge the stereotypical picture seen in American fiction.

References

Barthelme, D. "Lightning." In Forty Stories. New York: Penguin Books, 1987.
Bellow, S. The Adventures of Augie March. New York: Viking, 1953.
Bryant, D. Ella Price's Journal. Berkeley, Calif.: ATA Books, 1972.
Constantine, K. C. The Man Who Liked Slow Tomatoes. Boston: Godine, 1982.
Cunningham, P. "Own Your Advocacy." Adult Learning Magazine, Nov. 1990, p. 19.
French, M. The Women's Room. New York: Simon & Schuster, 1977.
Heilbrun, C. "Rage in a Tenured Position." Interview by Anne Matthews. New York Times Magazine, Nov. 8, 1992, pp. 8, 47.
Keillor, G. WLT: A Radio Romance. New York: Viking, 1991.
Kramer, J. E., Jr. The American College Novel. New York: Garland, 1981.
LaPaglia, N. Storytellers: The Image of the Two-Year College in American Fiction and in Women's Journals. DeKalb, Ill.: LEPS Press, Northern Illinois University, 1994.
Lyons, J. O. The College Novel in America. Carbondale, Ill.: Southern Illinois University Press, 1962.
Macaulay, B., and Gonzalez, V. The Institutional Wife Syndrome: A Metaphor Grounded in Reality. Paper presented at the 34th annual Adult Education Research Conference, University Park, Pa., 1993.
Mackin, E. The Nominative Case. New York: Walker, 1991.
McNeil, M. "Ordinary Women/Extraordinary Effort: African American Churchwomen as Leaders and Adult Educators, 1920–1940." Unpublished Ed.D. dissertation, Northern Illinois University, 1994.
Mason, B. A. "Shiloh." In Shiloh and Other Stories. New York: HarperCollins, 1982.
Moore, L. Anagrams. New York: Knopf, 1986.

National Lampoon's Animal House. Directed by John Landis, 1978. Motion picture.

Noble, B. P. "She Always *Said* Feminism and Economics Can Mix." *New York Times,* July 10, 1994, p. F7.

Oates, J. C. *Them.* New York: Ballantine, 1969.

Oates, J. C. "Angst." In *The Hungry Ghosts.* Los Angeles: Black Sparrow Press, 1975.

Pelletier, N. *The Rearrangement.* New York: Macmillan, 1985.

Schaeffer, S. F. *Falling.* New York: Macmillan, 1973.

Smith, P. *Killing the Spirit: Higher Education in America.* New York: Penguin Books, 1990.

Steinem, G. *Revolution from Within: A Book of Self-Esteem.* Boston: Little, Brown, 1992.

Walker, W. *The Immediate Prospect of Being Hanged.* New York: Viking, 1989.

Willeford, C. *Miami Blues.* New York: Ballantine: 1984.

Wong, J. S. *Fifth Chinese Daughter.* Seattle: University of Washington Press, 1989. (Originally published 1945.)

NANCY LAPAGLIA is professor of humanities at Richard J. Daley College, City Colleges of Chicago.

*Sexual harassment is one manifestation of abuse of power in the
academic environment. This phenomenon remains relatively
unexamined in the community college.*

Sexual Harassment in the Community College: The Abuse of Power

Robert O. Riggs, Patricia Hillman Murrell

In her novel, *Ella Price's Journal,* Dorothy Bryant (1972) chronicles the saga of
a young woman as she hesitatingly enrolls in Bay Junior College when her
daughter turns age 15. Ella Price experiences the seductive and transformative
power of the curriculum and instructional processes and eventually succumbs
to the amorous advances of Dan Harkan, her English professor. Twenty years
after the publication of this book, Ella Price's experience is apparently being
played out in real life in all too many instances in our nation's colleges.

Few issues appearing within the academy over the past two decades have
commanded the level and frequency of professional discourse accorded that
of sexual harassment. Since the early 1980s dozens of books, scores of institutional surveys and reports, and hundreds of professional articles have
addressed various aspects of this complex issue of sexual harassment.

In view of this intense level of discourse, the paucity of inquiry about sexual harassment in the community college sector is remarkable. We conducted
a thorough survey of the professional literature but failed to identify reports of
the incidence of sexual harassment on two-year campuses or professional articles considering how the unique characteristics of community colleges impact
on the issue of sexual harassment. This circumstance raises these questions: Is
sexual harassment less of a problem for two-year institutions than is the case
for four-year colleges? If so, what characteristics of the two-year campuses
shield them from the problem? Is the absence of research on this question simply a reflection of the lack of research on the community college generally?

In examining these questions, we first define sexual harassment and discuss its prevalence on college campuses. Next, we critique the pertinent theories that seek to explain or to predict harassing behavior and relate these to the

NEW DIRECTIONS FOR COMMUNITY COLLEGES, no. 89, Spring 1995 © Jossey-Bass Publishers community college context. Last, we address issues of professional practice and needed research initiatives related to the issue of sexual harassment on community college campuses.

What Is Sexual Harassment and How Prevalent Is It in Academe?

Sexual harassment includes demands for sexual favors in exchange for benefits (quid pro quo) or the creation of a hostile work or educational environment. Such harassment is a form of sex or gender discrimination, one of a group of civil rights violations against which all institutions must guard. Title VII of the Civil Rights Act of 1964 and Title IX of the Education Amendments of 1972 are the federal statutes under which are brought the majority of sexual harassment complaints against higher education institutions and their employees. The Civil Rights Act of 1991 provides additional remedies and redress to sexual harassment complainants.

Sexual harassment in an academic context has been defined by the National Advisory Council on Women's Educational Programs (quoted in Paludi, 1990, p. 3): "Academic sexual harassment is the use of authority to emphasize the sexuality or sexual identity of the student in a manner which prevents or impairs the student's full enjoyment of educational benefits, climate, or opportunity." It is this definition that is applied or used as we view Dan Harkan's impropriety in the case of Ella Price.

Sexual harassment can occur in a variety of permutations: persons of the same sex can harass, females can harass males, faculty members can harass colleagues, administrators can harass classified employees, and so on. However, the overwhelmingly prevalent pattern of sexual harassment on college campuses involves a male faculty member harassing a female student. It is this category of offenses, therefore, that serves as the focal point for this chapter, and the one that is illustrated by the story of Ella Price and her English professor.

A national survey conducted by the National Advisory Council for Women's Education Programs in 1980 was the first to query women college students whether they had ever experienced sexual advances from their professors and their responses to these behaviors (Bogart and Stein, 1987). Since that survey, many institutions have conducted in-house studies and produced statistical indicators depicting the scope of the problem. Dziech and Weiner (1990) reviewed a sample of surveys conducted between 1980 and 1983 at a variety of higher education institutions and concluded that despite variations in the surveys—formats, definitions, and sampling techniques—there appeared to be a consistent pattern of about 20 percent to 30 percent of women students who reported experiencing some form of sexual harassment during their college years.

Fitzgerald and Shullman (1993) call attention to the numerous reports that chronicle the extensive harassment of women in institutions of higher education. They conclude, "In sum, conservative estimates support that 1 of every

2 women will be harassed at some point during her academic or working life, indicating that sexual harassment is the most widespread of all forms of sexual victimization studied to date" (p. 8). Although the majority of these incidents will probably not match the severity of Ella Price's, others may result in even greater damage than she experienced.

These reports of the incidence of sexual harassment on college campuses as well as those others that appear in the professional literature are drawn from experiences on four-year campuses. Are these reports of the incidence and nature of sexual harassment also typical of the two-year college? As we indicated earlier, the answer to this question is not available in the higher education literature.

Perhaps the best available evidence regarding the possible incidence of sexual harassment on the community college campus can be gleaned from The Carnegie Foundation for the Advancement of Teaching's (1990) widely read report *Campus Life: In Search of Community.* The report delineates the results of 1989 national surveys of college and university presidents and chief student affairs officers. Presidents were asked, "During 1988–89, what three campus-life issues on your campus have given greatest concern?" (p. 138). For the aggregated sample (research and doctoral granting, comprehensive, liberal arts, and two-year), 2 percent of all presidents listed sexual harassment as one of the three most pressing issues. However, no two-year president identified sexual harassment as a most pressing campus issue. The presidents were also asked to gauge the severity of sexual harassment as a problem on their campuses. Forty percent of two-year presidents indicated that sexual harassment was not a problem on their campuses. By contrast, only 29 percent of all presidents responded in this manner.

Chief student affairs officers from the same institutional sample were also surveyed during 1989 in conjunction with the Carnegie study. Asked to rate the five-year change in sexual harassment as a campus life problem, respondents from the aggregated sample indicated that sexual harassment was not a problem for 26 percent of the campuses and less of a problem for 9 percent. The two-year campus respondents reported that sexual harassment was not a problem for 36 percent of the campus and less of a problem for 10 percent.

In short, two-year presidents and chief student affairs officers are aware of sexual harassment as a potential campus life problem. At the same time, their responses indicate they perceive the incidence of sexual harassment to be lower than that reported for four-year campuses. Given that sexual harassment is a reflection and manifestation of power imbalances between the harasser and the harassed, we can speculate about the likelihood of it occurring on two-year campuses by examining the concept of professorial power.

Power as a Theoretical Cause of Sexual Harassment

Community college faculty—whether they are titled teachers, instructors, faculty, or professors, irrespective of their tenure status, and with or without academic rank—are accorded unique positions of power and authority within their respective institutions. Although community college faculty members, viewed from a societal perspective, have lower social and economic status than their colleagues in research universities or prestigious liberal arts colleges, they do hold and exercise significant power relative to their students.

Community college professors can derive power from a variety of sources. Taken singly or in combination the following seven power bases can easily be seen as containing the potential for good or for mischief.

Expert power reflects the instructor's academic credentials, skill, and experience that can be used to foster students' academic and intellectual development.

Referent power is derived from the professor's personality and the degree to which he or she can stimulate admiration and affection from students who identify with him or her.

Legitimate power stems from the professor's role within the college. The professor by virtue of his or her status within the classroom automatically draws deference from his or her students.

Reward power speaks to the self-interests of students seeking grades, positive recommendations, or encouragement from their professors. To demonstrate integrity, reward power must be closely associated with performance.

Coercive power influences students through the professor's threat of punishment or withholding of grades, recommendations, and so on, because of particular student behaviors or absence of these behaviors.

Connection power stems from the instructor's association with others with whom students wish to or need to connect, for example, senior college officers, other instructors, and employers.

Information power lies in the professor's access to or possession of information that students value because it may affect their academic and professional goals.

French and Raven (1959) provide a classical paradigm of personal and corporate power that may be helpful in analyzing the possible misuses of power by community college faculty. The authors suggest two types of power: "socialized" power and "personalized" power. Socialized power is power exercised for the good of the college and for others within the college community. Professors' motivations and goals are aligned with those of the institution and academic unit. As professors employ socialized power, they look for win-win situations that will benefit students, the college, and themselves. They seek to empower students with a sense of collaboration and maturity so as to promote academic and personal development. Personalized power, however, is power used for self-enhancement and self-aggrandizement. Professors exercising personalized power seek to dominate others by intimidation and coercion; they strive for win-lose situations. They look at the collegiate environment as an opportunity to achieve personal success or rewards at the expense of students.

When a professor uses personalized power, students tend to feel submissive, manipulated, and peripheral.

When examined through the conceptual lenses of types of power and power bases, it is evident that the instructor occupies a forceful role. As elucidated by Zalk (1990), "The bottom line in the relationship between faculty member and student is *power*. The faculty member has it and the student does not. As intertwined as the faculty-student roles may be, and as much as one must exist for the other to exist, they are not equal collaborators. The student does not negotiate—indeed, has nothing to negotiate with" (p. 145). In essence, there is no equal bargaining position for the student; there is no quid pro quo in the strict legal sense. Zalk goes on to suggest that the lens needed to examine the professor's power bases must be a complex one because his (or her) power is both real and concrete—imagined and elusive.

Zalk recognizes the power of professors to award grades, to write employment recommendations, and to influence faculty colleagues' attitudes toward students. She also points out the professors' power manifested through superior knowledge and presumed wisdom. However, her most frightening observations relate to professors' power to enhance or diminish students' self-esteem and to contribute to the intellectual development of students. She writes, "Professors are expected to nurture a student's capacity to think analytically, to reason logically, to harness creativity, in short, to mature intellectually and aesthetically. This implies that the professor's power extends over the minds of his students" (p. 146).

This power can be lethal when combined with sexuality. As Dziech and Weiner indicate in *The Lecherous Professor* (1984), "Sexual harassment is a power issue, and the power of the professoriate is enormous" (p. 124).

Education can be and, we believe, should be transformational. That is what Zalk (1990) describes. She further assigns the role of bringing about that transformation to the faculty member, thus placing enormous power in his or her hands. It is the professor who chooses the curriculum and the content of the discipline with which the students engage. In the case of Ella Price, she was assigned novels to read—*The Scarlet Letter, Madame Bovary, Washington Square, Main Street, Candida, Metamorphosis, The Autobiography of Malcolm X, Anna Karenina*—all of which were assigned intentionally, and appropriately so, to challenge Ella's current thinking and create disequilibrium, a necessary condition if learning is to occur.

Dan Harkan then very consciously and intentionally turned his legitimate socialized power into personalized referent power to capitalize on the vulnerability inherent in Ella's transition. He took unfair advantage of the situation described in one of his own assigned readings by G. B. Shaw (1909): "You have learned something, and that always feels, at first, as if you had lost something." Ella was not assaulted or raped, at least not in the legal sense; she actively participated in arranging the trysts and never resisted her professor's sexual advances. But the relationship was never equal; Dan Harkan had the power—power over Ella Price's mind. He had the power of the curriculum, the power of his position in the institution, and the power to manipulate the process of teaching for his own ends. Whether this was his intention at the outset is immaterial; whether Ella encouraged his advances is of no consequence; he served as an emissary for the community college and he violated the trust that accrues to the professor in his or her role as agent of the institution.

Other Conceptual Models for Sexual Harassment

Tangri, Burt, and Johnson (1982) explore three explanatory models of sexual harassment at work that were derived from previous research, court cases, and legal defenses: the natural/biological model, the organizational model, and the sociocultural model. These models may provide further help in analyzing the causes of sexual harassment and issues of power on community college campuses.

The natural or biological model asserts that sexual harassment is simply a natural sexual attraction among people. This model has two aspects. The first posits that sexual harassing behavior is not meant as such, but is simply a natural expression of men's more powerful sex drives; the second version proposes no unequal sex drives, but stresses that any individual may be attracted to any other individual, and may pursue that attraction without intent to harass.

In adapting the natural/biological model to the community college context, one would expect harassing acts to resemble courtship behaviors, and the acts should stop if and when one party indicates disinterest or distaste. Given that the majority of community college students are female, the largest number of harassing acts would emanate from this group. Moreover, "victims," whether male or female, would be flattered, or at least not offended by these acts. Under this model "victims" would not be expected to file complaints or to perceive negative consequences as a result of the harassing behaviors. Clearly this model does not mirror the reality of harassing behavior on our campuses. The reality is that complaints are filed and the lives of victims of sexual harassment are damaged.

The organizational model holds that institutions may provide an opportunity structure that makes sexual harassment possible. Because community colleges are characterized by vertical stratification, persons in superior positions can use their power to extort sexual gratification from their subordinates. Under this model those persons holding lower levels of power within the organization would be most vulnerable to harassing behavior. This asymmetrical relationship between superordinates and subordinates deprives subordinates of the material independence and security necessary to resist sexual harassment.

In this model the ratio of males to females can facilitate or inhibit sexual harassment, and the greater the differential power in the organization or the higher the status of the harasser the more severe and frequent the acts of sexual harassment. Thus in the community college one would not expect much harassment of faculty by other faculty because the ratio of male to female faculty is essentially equal. Similarly, the ratio of male faculty to female students might provide some safety to women students because they are in the majority. There are also many same-sex faculty members for students of either sex to approach about having been harassed. Even among administrators, in the community college there are more female administrators than in other types of institutions of higher education. In sum, the application of the organizational model to the community college might suggest a lower incidence of sexual harassment than would be present in other institutional contexts.

The third model, the sociocultural model, posits that sexual harassment is one manifestation of the larger patriarchal system in which men rule and social benefits legitimize their power. It suggests that members of each sex are socialized to play their respective roles. Males are rewarded by society for aggressive behavior and domineering sexual behaviors and females are rewarded for passivity and acquiescence. The model postulates that male gender is a better predictor of who will harass than organizational position, and that women, because of their relative powerlessness and sex role socialization, are more likely to be victims. Therefore, under this model female students within the community college would be most vulnerable to sexual harassment by male professors.

Gutek and Morasch (1982) have proposed a "sex-role spillover" explanatory model for sexual harassment. The model proposes that when organizations are dominated by one sex or the other, the gender of the predominant group influences the work role expectations for particular positions and the treatment of women within the work environment.

In male-dominated professional fields, the traditional role of women as subordinate to men is facilitated by the dearth of women in power within the organizations. Men react to women at work as they do toward women in their personal lives, and women accommodate this request. In this scenario conditional sex roles are "spilled over" and reinforced in the work setting. Consequently, the model's major forecast would suggest that gender-balanced work groups would encounter less sexual harassment. In the community college where the majority of students are female and women are more fully represented among the faculty and throughout the administrative hierarchy, less harassment might be predicted.

In attempting to apply any of these theoretical explanations of sexual harassment to the community college context, it is important to observe that as institutions of higher education, community colleges differ in significant ways from four-year colleges and universities. These differences in institutional mission, academic programs, student and faculty characteristics, and so on, may make community colleges especially vulnerable to the problem of sexual harassment.

Murrell, Riggs, and Williford (in press) critique the nature of community college institutional cultures, students, and faculties as they relate to the issue of sexual harassment, and they observe, "Taken together, these considerations [community college cultures, faculties, and students] may portend a lack of cultural identity and a weakened sense of community when compared with traditional academic environments. In such a climate, both faculty and students need enhanced skills to avoid abuse and exploitation" (p. 11). Similarly, one two-year chief executive officer, Constance Carroll (1993), president of San Diego Mesa College, believes sexual harassment on college campuses is a product of systemic oppression and institutionally structured domination and subordination of women. She writes, "Because most members of a college community have been socialized within a culture that has a history of sexism, and because academe itself has a similar tradition, administrators must take affirmative steps to educate themselves and campus community members regarding appropriate and inappropriate behavior" (p. 25).

The delicate faculty-student relationship is a critical factor in success at college. If it is soiled by abuse and sexual harassment, whatever the theoretical explanation, a student may be too frightened to complain and may withdraw from school or may be charmed into seduction, as was the case with Ella Price. Neither community colleges nor society at large can afford either of these outcomes.

Implications for Research and Practice

Any attempt to pull these theoretical models into a meaningful pattern must be tempered by the knowledge that they are based on conditions present in four-year institutions and nonacademic organizations. Theory must be tested by observation and empirical data—information that is not currently available for the community college sector. Moreover, the impressions of the presidents and chief student affairs officers surveyed by the Carnegie Foundation (1990) can neither be supported nor questioned due to the absence of hard data. Consequently, the first priority for community college leaders is to ascertain the frequency and types of sexual harassment that may be occurring on their campuses. A number of proven methods and instruments for this purpose are reported in the professional literature. Of particular note is Fitzgerald, Drasgow, and Gelfand's (1993) Sexual Experience Questionnaire. This is the most widely employed instrument for assessing sexual harassment of students by professors, and because of its frequent application, data collected using this survey could be readily compared with those collected by other colleges and universities.

A second priority for two-year institutions is to ensure that appropriate policies and procedures that declare sexual harassment illegal and facilitate its prevention are in place. The most comprehensive study of sexual harassment policies and procedures at institutions of higher education was conducted by Robertson, Dyer, and Campbell (1988). The authors report that among the surveyed public two- and four-year public institutions only 79.9 percent had sexual harassment policies and only 54.2 percent had grievance procedures. Because the law mandates and good professional practice demands that institutions have sexual harassment policies and procedures in place, the fact that a number of institutions report they are not in compliance is alarming. Institutions without such policies and procedures should move expeditiously to correct this shortcoming. A number of helpful guides for the development and implementation of sexual harassment policies and procedures for college campuses are available (American Council on Education, 1986; Riggs, Murrell, and Cutting, 1993).

Three other areas of research emphasis have been identified by Fitzgerald and Shullman (1993) that may have import for two-year colleges. The authors suggest that institutions, in their haste to develop policies and procedures to address sexual harassment, have not given thoughtful attention to needs analysis, goals specifications, and the development and assessment of outcome criteria. Training programs have been developed without an articulated conceptual framework or any information concerning their impact and effectiveness. The authors call for examinations of organizational reactions to the presence of sexual harassment and state, "The proposition that workplace norms or organizational climate can inhibit sexual harassment is extremely promising and offers immediate targets for practical interventions" (p. 15). They propose that sexual harassment is much too widespread to be completely accounted for by individual sexual deviance or desire for gratification; rather the importance of organizational factors prominent in the stimulating or inhibiting of harassment represents great potential for investigation.

Sexual harassment is a national problem of alarming magnitude with destructive human consequences. The problem is a complex function of individual and organizational factors, of personal and corporate power, of organizational and job context and culture, and of individual vulnerability, response, and motive. All of these considerations are present on community college campuses, yet sexual harassment has not received the degree of attention on two-year campuses that seems commensurate with the apparent gravity of the problem. The initiation of professional discourse concerning this issue is long overdue.

In many ways Ella Price was well served by the community college. She was provided access to an education she had spurned earlier in favor of marriage. She had the opportunity to achieve confidence in her ability and develop her identity, ultimately gaining the self-possession and assurance to liberate herself from a suffocating marriage relationship. Community colleges do a marvelous job for thousands of students day in and day out, year after year, meeting both their developmental and instrumental needs. The system usually works. What went wrong for Ella Price was that one faculty member, with the institution's tacit concurrence, abused his power and manipulated and violated a student during a very vulnerable transitional period.

Community college leaders must ensure that an environment of respect and compassion exists on their campuses. They have an obligation to embrace diversity and create a climate of inclusiveness, free of harassment. In so doing, they can make sure that the fictional experiences of Ella Price do not become a reality.

References

American Council on Education. *Sexual Harassment on Campus: Suggestions for Reviewing Campus Policy and Educational Programs.* Washington, D.C.: American Council on Education, Dec. 1986.

Bogart, K., and Stein, N. "Breaking the Silence: Sexual Harassment in Education." *Sex Equity and Sexuality in Education,* 1987, pp. 146–163.

Bryant, D. *Ella Price's Journal.* Berkeley, Calif.: ATA Books, 1972.

Carnegie Foundation for the Advancement of Teaching. *Campus Life: In Search of Community.* Lawrenceville, N.J.: Princeton University Press, 1990.

Carroll, C. "Sexual Harassment on Campus: Enhancing Awareness and Promoting Change." *Educational Record,* 1993, 74 (1), 21–26.

Dziech, B. W., and Weiner, L. *The Lecherous Professor: Sexual Harassment on Campus.* Boston: Beacon Press, 1984.

Dziech, B. W., and Weiner, L. *The Lecherous Professor: Sexual Harassment on Campus* (2nd ed.). Boston: Beacon Press, 1990.

Fitzgerald, L. F., Drasgow, F., and Gelfand, M. *Sexual Experience Questionnaire, Form W (E).* Unpublished manuscript, 1993.

Fitzgerald, L. F., and Shullman, S. L. "Sexual Harassment: A Research Analysis and Agenda for the 1990's." *Journal of Vocational Behavior,* 1993, 42, 5–27.

French, J., and Raven, B. "The Bases of Social Power," In D. Cartwright (ed.), *Studies in Social Power.* Ann Arbor: Institute for Social Research, University of Michigan, 1959.

Gutek, B. A., and Morasch, B. "Sex-Ratios, Sex-Role Spillover, and Sexual Harassment of Women at Work." *Journal of Social Issues,* 1982, 38 (4), 55–74.

Murrell, P. H., Riggs, R. O., and Williford, L. C. "Sexual Harassment of Female Students: Implications for Community College Practices." *Community College Journal of Research and Practice,* in press.

Paludi, M. A. (ed.). "The Student in the Back Row: Avoiding Sexual Harassment in the Classroom." In *Ivory Power: Sexual Harassment on Campus.* Albany: State University of New York Press, 1990.

Riggs, R. O., Murrell, P. H., and Cutting, J. C. *Sexual Harassment in Higher Education: From Conflict to Community.* 1993 ASHE-ERIC Higher Education Reports, Report Two. Washington, D.C.: Association for the Study of Higher Education, 1993.

Robertson, C., Dyer, C. C., and Campbell, D. A. "Campus Harassment: Sexual Harassment Policies and Procedures at Institutions of Higher Learning." *Signs,* 1988, 13, 792–812.

Shaw, G. B. *Major Barbara.* London: A. Constable, 1909.

Tangri, S. S., Burt, M. R., and Johnson, L. B. "Sexual Harassment at Work: Three Explanatory Models." *Journal of Social Issues,* 1982, 38 (4), 33–54.

Zalk, S. R. "Men in the Academy: A Psychological Profile of Harassment." In M. Paludi (ed.), *Ivory Power: Sexual Harassment on Campus.* Albany: State University of New York Press, 1990.

ROBERT O. RIGGS is regents professor of higher education in the Department of Leadership at the University of Memphis and senior associate at the Center for the Study of Higher Education.

PATRICIA HILLMAN MURRELL is director of the Center for the Study of Higher Education and professor of higher education in the Department of Leadership at the University of Memphis.

The strong and colorful images that have characterized leadership in the two-year college are examined, and their impact on women and minorities and the effectiveness of community colleges is discussed.

Gendered Images of Community College Leadership: What Messages They Send

Susan B. Twombly

The junior college movement is "an army of struggling frontiersmen put together by General Koos and Colonels Eells and Campbell who then led them into all parts of the country . . . (Zook in Brint and Karabel, 1989, p. 35).

These times [the 1960s] demanded builders, political persuaders, organizers and master plan developers (Roueche, Baker, and Rose, 1989, p. 40).

Leaders, like athletes, are bigger, stronger, quicker, and better coached than ever. A generation of community college lore is available to current and upcoming leaders, and the smart ones are using it. . . . Somewhere out there is another Priest, another Cosand, and another Fordyce (Parish, 1988, p. 1).

Individuals in administrative positions must be concerned with (1) boundary spanning, not boundary defending, (2) empowering people, not controlling them, (3) working cooperatively, not competitively, (4) focusing on process, not product, (5) organizational flexibility, not rigidity, (6) quality, not quantity, (7) sharing information, not guarding it, and (8) creativity or intuition, not primarily rationality (Baker, 1994, pp. xv–xvi).

These few quotations provide a taste of just some of the colorful imagery characteristic of the two-year college literature on leadership. These images not only describe leadership behaviors, but even more importantly they serve as guides or standards for what leaders should do and who can qualify for leadership positions. Thus they serve as a kind of filter or screen. Think for a moment about the characteristics of a person who could fit the images described. Which, if any, of these images brings to mind women leaders? For that matter, what do the images imply about the leadership behavior of anyone who would occupy a leadership position?

Heralded as the democratizing force in higher education, community colleges have been slow to shed their image as top-down bureaucracies. They have also been slow to bring women and minorities into top leadership positions in proportion to their representation as faculty and students. Images of commanders, builders, managers, heroes, blue chippers, and visionaries may have reflected real needs during the growth and maturing stages of community college development, but today they may restrict who is considered for leadership positions. As community colleges face new organizational challenges, will new images be created that are more welcoming of the wide range of talent which must be considered to fill this leadership gap?

I argue here that the leadership literature, through the images it portrays, sets expectations and creates possibilities about who can be leaders. The images become norms or standards which, when matched with prevalent societal stereotypes about gender or members of other marginalized groups, serve either as barriers or as tickets to advancement. Leadership behaviors and qualities sought in new leaders in community colleges, as in all organizations, are influenced by context and the particular demands of social and historical situations (Selznick, 1984). In addition, beliefs and resulting images about the kind of leadership called for and the characteristics required in those who assume leadership positions also shape and constrain ideas about acceptable leadership (Amey and Twombly, 1992). Images of leadership are not merely neutral descriptors; they are gendered. Images acting as norms determine who has access to power and the nature of power a person can exercise. Therefore, it is important to expose and question the prevalent images. These images are found in many sources, but primarily in the published literature of the important spokespersons of the community college movement. And like the great leaders there have been relatively few of these individuals. In the next section I illustrate this point through an historical approach to gendered images. Through this approach it is easy to see how these images developed and have been perpetuated. Then I examine some of the recent writings on leadership to see if, in fact, the language has changed. Finally, I discuss more fully the implications of these images for women and minorities and for future leadership of community colleges.

Gendered Images: A Historical Perspective

The Early Years: 1900–1930s. The "great man" theory of leadership dominated during this early period in the development of community colleges. The literature is replete with accounts of how a few prominent university presidents, William Rainey Harper, Henry Tappan, and David Starr Jordan, supported the idea of the junior college and how a few university professors, Leonard Koos, Walter Eells, and Doak Campbell, imbued with a missionary zeal and progressive concern for improving society, almost single-handedly brought to life and shaped this new educational option (Brint and Karabel, 1989; Goodwin, 1971).

Of particular interest is how authors constructed junior colleges and their leaders in frontier, pioneer, and military images. In 1947 Zook, chief author of the *President's Commission on Higher Education Report,* described the junior college movement of the 1940s "as an army of struggling frontiersmen put together by General Koos and Colonels Eells and Campbell, who then led them to all parts of the country . . ." (Brint and Karabel, 1989, p. 35). Brint and Karabel (1989) reinforced the military images by describing Koos, Eells, and Campbell as "'intellectual commanders,'" the vanguard, who led their recruits to fight many battles . . ." (p. 35). According to Brint and Karabel, these men were truly transformational leaders. They created a paradigm for the junior college, tried to transform its primary mission from transfer function to vocational against the wishes of students and their parents, and groomed a successor generation of great leaders whose names still occupy a very important place in the community college movement, men such as S. V. Martorana, Leland Medsker, Raymond Schultz, and Edmund Gleazer.

These men were not individual institutional leaders, however. They exerted influence from their positions as university professors or, in the case of Campbell and Gleazer, as presidents of the American Association of Junior Colleges. Several factors affected early institutional leaders, notably the newness of the two-year college and its status as part of the public school system. Heads of private junior colleges, of which there were many in this early period, typically held the title of president; early public junior college leaders held the title of dean and reported to the superintendent of schools (Brothers, 1928; Green in Eells, 1931; Lee and Rosentengel, 1938). The descriptor applied to these early deans was that of errand boy (Johnson and Carpenter, 1943). In contrast to the image of commander or pioneer, errand boy deans were not overburdened with responsibilities and were not given much latitude in critical areas of policymaking (Johnson and Carpenter, 1943).

Independence: 1940s–1950s. In the 1940s and 1950s, a change in the imagery describing desirable and actual leadership practices began to occur. Tillery and Deegan (1985) described these years as the period during which leaders began to seek college identity and to gain independence from the secondary schools.

By the 1950s, the dean had been replaced by a president who assumed more and more responsibility. Pierce (1951) noted, "It appears, then, that junior colleges are coming more and more to have two general administrative officers, a chief administrator most often called 'president' and a second in command called 'dean'; and with the line-and-staff administrative organization, the other administrative officers are usually co-ordinates of equal rank serving under the leadership of the president and the dean" (p. 36). The ideal president of the emerging independent colleges was variously described as being in control but not being autocratic and as having inspirational qualities. Bogue (1950) used the analogies of the star who appears on stage, the gamey athlete, the courageous sea captain, the baseball player who "steps into the ball" (p. 299). Wartime metaphors were not lost on Bartky (1957), who described the leader of a junior college as one who must perform as the commander of a well-trained battleship.

Thus, during this period of independence, the focus shifted to institutional leaders and the skills necessary to achieve independence. The imagery of commander, gamey athlete, and kingpin coincided with the stage in the life cycle of junior/community colleges in which the struggle for independence dominated other considerations. Junior college authors seem to have seen this extremely active, even domineering, "great man" leadership style as necessary to accomplish the separation of junior colleges from the public schools and to fulfill what George Vaughan has called its "manifest destiny" (Vaughan, 1986).

Maturation: 1960s–1970s. During the 1960s, junior colleges entered a period of growth and maturation. Many of the present-day community colleges were born and junior colleges became community colleges. Not unexpectedly, images of leaders as commander and great man continued to dominate as strong leadership was thought necessary to build and develop community colleges out of relatively small junior colleges. Many of the characteristics once attributed to the national leaders of the two-year college movement, characteristics such as inspiration and pioneering spirit, became part of the rhetoric used to describe institutional leaders as well.

Many new presidents approached their positions in this pioneering tradition. Roueche, Baker, and Rose (1989) described the 1960s as "times [that] demanded builders, political persuaders, organizers, and master plan developers" (p. 40). Descriptors such as competitive, innovative, fast-moving, flexible, calculated risk takers, tough, dominating, and playing to win appear in the literature in reference to this time period (Brint and Karabel, 1989; Tillery Deegan, 1985). Barber (1992) described the founding president of Central Piedmont Community College as a transactional leader favoring centralized authority and control, paternalistic in his control over the budget, and coercive in his use of power. Even as community colleges developed more sophisticated administrative structures, a preference for strong, centralized, authoritarian power dominated (Alfred and Smydra, 1985).

By 1972 Richardson, Blocker, and Bender were advocating shared governance in light of what they termed "autocratic leaders [and] rigid bureaucracy" (p. v). The commander had become an autocrat, a negative image. However, the call for shared governance proved to be a brief interlude in the pursuit of the "great man" ideal of leadership. Although the terms changed during the 1960s to the 1980s, the ideal of strong leadership remained dominant (Amey and Twombly, 1992).

Recent Images: 1980s. While founding presidents of the 1960s were required to be visionaries, the later stages of the 1960s and early 1970s demanded efficient managers. The manager-leader turned his or her attention inward to using resources effectively. Some authors have suggested that slowed growth and managerial emphasis of the late 1970s resulted in myopic vision (Roueche, Baker, and Rose, 1989). The challenge, then, for leaders in maturing community colleges of the 1980s was renewal, the revitalizing of mature organizations. The model of leadership proposed was that of the transformational leader (Roueche, Baker, and Rose, 1989). In their influential book, *Shared Vision: Transformational Leadership in American Community Colleges,* Roueche, Baker, and Rose (1989) chose to label preferred leadership behaviors "transformational" and the people who exemplified these skills as "blue chippers." Transformational leadership relies on a "single, highly visible individual" who then communicates a vision persuasively down to the community (Bensimon, Neumann, and Birnbaum, 1989). Thus transformational leadership is really a version of the "great man" theory of leadership.

Roueche, Baker, and Rose (1989) were not alone in their inability to re-vision leadership for the future of community colleges. The theme dominating the late 1980s was the need to renew and avoid organizational decline. However, the type of leadership needed to accomplish this was not so clear as it had been in early periods in the life cycle of community colleges. Some authors proposed "image-neutral" activities such as interpreting the mission, managing the institution, creating the campus climate, and serving as educational leader (Vaughan, 1986). Others called for collaborative leadership (for example, Keyser, 1988).

Others reinforced the old imagery of the "great man" thinly disguised. Jacob (1989) invoked military images when he wrote of leaders who need to "marshal" community support and "join forces" with community organizations). *Leadership Abstracts,* a publication of the League for Innovation in the Community College, reprinted a list of leadership traits from *U.S. News and World Report* and deemed them appropriate for the community college leader of the twenty-first century. This list included such terms as "Master of Technology" and the "leader/motivator" who is also coach (Doucette, 1988). Although the leadership behaviors cited seem appropriate for an institution moving toward renewal, the repeated use of male pronouns, male-only examples (Doucette uses only male examples), and military and athletic metaphors project an image that continues to be exclusionary. We are reminded also of Parrish's plea (1988), cited at the beginning of this chapter, to find new leaders like the old ones, steeped in community college lore.

Amey and Twombly (1992) offer the interpretation that community college leaders recognize the skills necessary for mature colleges entering the twenty-first century are not those of the "great man," top-down leadership style. However, these leaders are reluctant to relinquish the heroic images so ingrained in the literature and in the minds of scholars.

Alternative Voices. Alternative images have been and continue to be present, although occupying a marginal place in the literature. Most alternative images have been voiced by feminists and often emerge from pieces written specifically about women.

Most of the alternative voices have come from the National Institute for Leadership Development and the American Association of Women in Community Colleges. The goal of the National Institute for Leadership Development is to promote a new model of leadership, that is, leadership based on inclusiveness, intuition, and horizontal connectedness rather than hierarchy. Relying heavily on the work of Carol Gilligan and works of her colleagues such as Belenky, Clinchy, Goldberger, and Tarule (1986), the National Institute for Leadership development assumes that most women's leadership style and preferences are different from men's and stresses development of the whole person. The *Journal of the American Association of Women in Community College* (AAWCC) has provided the most consistent forum for alternative images of leadership. The image of leadership reflected in several recent issues is that of connectedness, cooperation, and "webs and nets" rather than pyramids and hierarchical ladders. Unfortunately, this journal is not widely subscribed to, and thus the voices and images portrayed therein are marginalized or not well known.

Mainstream writers such as Roueche, Baker, and Rose (1989) and Vaughan (1989) devote specific chapters to women leaders in their respective books about community college leaders. The Roueche, Baker, and Rose study of transformational leaders includes a chapter devoted to the women "blue chippers" and the other women leaders in their study. This chapter, authored by a woman who is not included as a major author of the book, makes an important contribution. A comparison of men and women on various dimensions of leadership suggested there really are few major differences in leadership style and ability among effective leaders.

Vaughan also makes a contribution by drawing attention to women leaders—presidents. However, much attention is paid to the problems women face in leadership positions. Vaughan reports that the presidency is viewed as asexual by incumbents.

New Images

There is some hope that images of leadership are changing. In addition to the alternative voices which have, at best, been just that, two recent examples suggest the rhetoric, and thus the images, of leadership are changing to fit the needs of community colleges in the final years of the twentieth century. These examples are notable both for what they say and for who wrote them. The first set of examples comes from *Cultural Leadership: Inside America's Community Colleges* (1992), edited by George Baker, and the second from *A Handbook on the Community College in America* (1994), also edited by Baker. The central focus of the first book is that a holistic, cultural approach to leading and managing the community college is necessary. A new paradigm of the learning community is offered. Terms such as "empowering leadership teams" (p. x) enter the realm of desirable practice. According to Baker, "Leaders shape behavior in others by . . . coaching, teaching, and role modeling. Leaders increase motivation, satisfaction, and performance through the allocation of status and rewards. . . . While effective founding presidents were often charismatic and autocratic, the new leaders will need to be inspirational and participative" (p. x). This is very different from what seems to be an almost desperate plea of Parrish (1988) to recover the old lore and leadership style of yesterday.

Two of the book's more interesting chapters, both written by Barber (1992a, 1992b), are case studies of two leaders, a founding president and his successor, a woman. This approach highlights the contingent nature of leadership: different styles are appropriate at different times, but its relevance here is that the successor president, who assumed the office in 1986, was a woman who used very different language in her remarks to the college community. She used words such as vision, commitment, caring, and competence. She talked about "vigor and student centeredness, instructional excellence, and dedication to meeting the needs of students" (p. 165). She talked about her family. As Barber says, "For Central Piedmont, the announcement, the event, and Shaw's videotaped remarks signaled the beginning of the reframing process. The language of her remarks suggested some new basic assumptions, for example, about the nature of reality and truth ('analytical'), human relationships ('sharing'), human activity ('teamwork'), and human nature ('helping others achieve')" (p. 166).

In the second book, Baker (1994) introduces the section on leading and managing by outlining the tasks of administrators quoted at the beginning of this chapter: "(1) boundary spanning, not boundary defending, (2) empowering people, not controlling them, (3) working cooperatively, not competitively, (4) focusing on process, not product, (5) organizational flexibility, not rigidity, (6) quality, not quantity, (7) sharing information, not guarding it, and (8) creativity or intuition, not primarily rationality" (p. xvi). These themes are echoed throughout the seven chapters that deal with leadership and management issues.

These two examples are important for several reasons. In addition to the messages communicated about appropriate leadership for the twentieth-first century, the location and authorship of these recent chapters is important. The majority of the chapter authors for the first book, *Cultural Leadership* (Baker, 1992), are women and most represent new names in the world of writing about leadership in community colleges. The *Handbook* section on leading and managing community colleges is less representative in this respect. However, the *Handbook* (Baker, 1992) itself is a very prestigious book and will likely receive widespread use. Thus the images communicated about leadership in this outlet are important.

Implications for Women and Minorities

In this chapter and elsewhere (Amey and Twombly, 1992), I have argued that leadership behaviors exemplified in the images of a "General" Koos and "Colonel" Eells have dominated as the preferred leadership style in the community college movement. The strong, often militaristic or athletic descriptors used have perpetuated the "great man" theory of leadership, even when authors such as John Roueche and others (1989) have recognized the need for a different type of leadership. Through the 1980s writers such as Deegan and Tillery (1985), Parrish (1988), and Brint and Karabel (1989) continued to reinforce this "great man" view by repeatedly exalting the achievements of the few great leaders who shaped the movement.

Through the 1980s, there were only a few alternative voices such as the *Journal of the American Association of Women in Community and Junior Colleges* or the National Institute for Leadership Development that provided images of leaders as teachers, weavers, empowerers, or collaborators.

What are the effects of the imagery used? Recent presidential campaigns have taught us well about the important role and uses of images. Although the images used to describe community college leadership do not explicitly express a preference for one gender or the other, the message is implicit. One consequence of imagery is its unspoken exclusion of individuals who do not fit the images and the marginalization of writers who do not use the same language. A thorough study of the literature led Amey and Twombly (1992) to conclude, "Images of appropriate leadership in community colleges and societal stereotypes about the proper role of women have made it difficult to envision women in the role of leaders" (p. 408). The relationship of leadership images to gender is complicated. Thinking back to the images recounted in this chapter, we would probably agree that women do not easily fit. Moreover, perpetuating the idea that community colleges need strong, individual leaders who are commanders of their ships would serve to exclude those women and others, including many men, who prefer an alternative leadership style. However, when the word *asexual* is used to describe the presidency (for example, Vaughan, 1986), the unique qualities that women might offer to leadership are denied. Advocating for alternative stereotypically feminine images, such as nurturer, runs the risk of creating other types of equally exclusionary images.

Until the two recent books edited by Baker (1992, 1994) promoted such potentially neutral images as collaborator, the alternative voices in the community college literature have been largely based on the work of Gilligan (1982). Gilligan's work, although making an extremely important contribution to gender studies, suggests men and women are essentially different and that women (presumably all women) are nurturing and caring and prefer connection and collaboration whereas all men prefer hierarchy, power, and war. Furthermore, the assumption is made by many authors who use Gilligan's work that the leadership qualities offered by women are better than those of men.

There are a couple of problems with such views. They run the risk of creating the image that women are "soft" and value relationships over decision making. However, more importantly, more damagingly, these alternative voices argue for essential, unbridgeable differences between men and women making alternative images for leadership not tied to a particular gender stereotypes difficult to establish.

What little research exists on this topic supports a more gender inclusive interpretation. Based on a study of effective presidents, Gillett-Karam (1989) concluded that effective leadership is a "concept relating attributes of community college presidents without reference to their sex" (p. 255). She found relatively few major differences between women and men on major dimensions of leadership behavior. Cimperman (1986), in a study of the self-perceptions of male and female Wisconsin community college leaders, and Jones (1985) both found few real differences in leadership styles among community college leaders despite biographical differences. These findings are consistent with Epstein's (1988) and Tavris's (1992) conclusion after reviewing much of the gender research of the 1970s and 1980s that gender differences are socially constructed not empirically "real." Rather, they argue, because of how gender and gender relations are socially constructed, we persist in believing there are differences. We perpetuate these differences in our language, writing, symbols, and images. As this chapter has demonstrated, community colleges have effectively perpetuated strong differences through images. It is difficult for women to measure up to these images. It is an even more difficult challenge to create images that are more inclusive.

Even when women do gain access to community college leadership positions, their accomplishments are sometimes marginalized or discussed in terms of problems rather than potential. Writing about the community college presidency, Vaughan (1989) states, "Trustees are obligated to determine the right fit, or chemistry for a college at a particular time and location. There are some cases when the right fit requires a white male president and other cases when it requires a female president" (p. 76). These words dramatically reinforce the role of image, in this case gender.

Can community colleges, with their diverse constituencies, afford to maintain narrow, exclusionary images of leadership? Equally important, will the "great man" model of leadership serve the community colleges well? George Baker (1992, 1994) has answered these questions with a resounding "no." The terms in which leadership is discussed in these two major edited volumes seem to be truly more gender neutral as well as more in tune with the types of skills necessary for dramatically changing conditions. Now that such characteristics as collaboration, team building, process orientation, flexibility, creativity, and intuition have entered the mainstream, the challenge seems to be one of coining clever images that can compete with the likes of "general" and "commander."

References

Alfred, R. L., and Smydra, D. F. "Reforming Governance, Resolving Challenges to Institutional Authority." In W. L. Deegan, D. Tillery, and Associates (eds.), *Renewing the American Community College*. San Francisco: Jossey-Bass, 1985.

Amey, M. J., and Twombly, S. B. "Re-Visioning Leadership in Community Colleges." *Review of Higher Education*, 1992, *15* (2), 125–150.

Baker, G. A., III (ed.). *Cultural Leadership: Inside America's Community Colleges.* Washington, D.C.: American Association of Community and Junior Colleges, 1992.

Baker, G. A., III (ed.). *A Handbook on the Community College in America: Its History, Mission, and Management.* Westport, Conn.: Greenwood Press, 1994.

Barber, P. "Cultural Leadership: The Founder." In G. A. Baker (ed.), *Cultural Leadership: Inside America's Community Colleges.* Washington, D.C.: American Association of Community and Junior Colleges, 1992a.

Barber, P. "Cultural Leadership: The Successor." In G. A. Baker (ed.), *Cultural Leadership: Inside America's Community Colleges.* Washington, D.C.: American Association of Community and Junior Colleges, 1992b.

Bartky, J. "The Nature of Junior College Administration." *Junior College Journal,* 1957, *28,* 3–7.

Belenky, M., Clinchy, B., Goldberger, N., and Tarule, J. *Women's Ways of Knowing.* New York: Basic Books, 1986.

Bensimon, E. M., Neumann, A., and Birnbaum, R. *Making Sense of Administrative Leadership: The 'L' Word in Higher Education: ASHE-ERIC Higher Education Report no. 1.* Washington, D.C.: School of Education and Human Development, George Washington University, 1989.

Bogue, J. P. *The Community College.* New York: McGraw-Hill, 1950.

Brint, S., and Karabel, J. *The Diverted Dream: Community Colleges and the Promise of Educational Opportunity in America, 1900–1985.* New York: Oxford University Press, 1989.

Brothers, E. Q. "Present Day Practices and Tendencies in the Administration and Organization of Public Junior Colleges." *School Review,* 1928, *36,* 665–674.

Cimperman, R. "Women in Leadership Roles: A Field Study of Women Administrators' Perceptions of Self," 1986. (ED 269 872).

Doucette, D. (ed.). "The 21st Century Executive." *Leadership Abstracts,* 1988, *1,* 1–21. (ED 302 294)

Eells, W. C. *The Junior College.* Boston: Houghton Mifflin, 1931.

Epstein, C. *Deceptive Distinctions: Sex, Gender, and the Social Structure.* New Haven: Yale University Press and New York: Russell Sage Foundation, 1988.

Gillett-Karam, R. "Women in Leadership Roles." In J. Roueche, G. Baker, III, and R. Rose, *Shared Vision: Transformational Leadership in American Community Colleges.* Washington, D.C.: Community College Press and American Association of Community Junior Colleges, 1989.

Gilligan, C. *In a Different Voice.* Cambridge, Mass: Harvard University Press, 1982.

Goodwin, G. L. "The Historical Development of the Community-Junior College Ideology." Doctoral dissertation. University of Illinois, Urbana, 1971.

Jacob, J. E. "Education and Revitalization of Urban America." *Leadership Abstracts* 2 (19), not paginated. (Newsletter of the League for Innovation in the Community College.)

Johnson, J. R., and Carpenter, W. W. "Dean or Errand Boy?" *Junior College Journal,* 1943, *13,* 381–383.

Jones, S. "Determining the Impact of Biographical and Situational Variables on the Leadership Styles and Effectiveness of Community/Junior College Administrators," 1985. ERIC Doc (ED 272 251).

Keyser, J. S. "Collaborative Decision-Making." *Leadership Abstracts,* 1988, *1* (17), not paginated. Newsletter of the League for Innovation in the Community College.

Lee, C., and Rosentengel, W. E. "Philosophy of Junior College Administration," *Junior College Journal,* 1938, *8,* 227–230.

Parrish, J. H. "Individual and Group Responsibility for Leadership Development." *Leadership Abstracts,* 1988, *1*(7), not paginated, Newsletter of the League for Innovation in the Community College.

Pierce, A. C. "Deans in the Organization and Administration of Junior Colleges." *Junior College Journal,* 1951, *21,* 364–366.

Richardson, R. C., Blocker, C. E., and Bender, L. W. *Governance for the Two-Year College.* Englewood Cliffs, N.J.: Prentice Hall, 1972.

Roueche, J. E., Baker, G. A., and Rose, R. R. *Shared Vision: Transformational Leadership in American Community Colleges.* Washington, D.C.: Community College Press and American Association of Community and Junior Colleges, 1989.

Selznick, P. *Leadership in Administration.* Berkeley: University of California Press, 1984.

Tavris, C. *The Mismeasure of Woman.* New York: Simon & Schuster, 1992.

Tillery, D., and Deegan, W. L. "The Evolution of Two-Year Colleges Through Four Generations." In D. Tillery and W. L. Deegan (eds.), *Renewing the American Community College: Priorities and Strategies for Effective Leadership.* San Francisco: Jossey-Bass, 1985.

Vaughan, G. B. *The Community College Presidency.* New York: ACE/Macmillan, 1986.

Vaughan, G. B. (ed). *Leadership in Transition: The Community College Presidency.* New York: ACE/Macmillan, 1989.

SUSAN B. TWOMBLY is associate professor and department chairperson, Department of Educational Policy and Leadership, University of Kansas, Lawrence.

This chapter analyzes the impact of women on the community college presidency and their potential to make a unique contribution by connecting the characteristic strengths of their gender to the power of their office.

Women and the Community College Presidency: Challenges and Possibilities

Deborah M. DiCroce

"Few things that can happen to a nation are more important than the invention of a new form of verse." So declared twentieth-century English poet T. S. Eliot (1927, p. xii). As part of my presidential inaugural address in September 1989, I used this quote to illustrate the dramatic effect the community college has had on American higher education. Now, almost six years later, I return to Eliot's words to establish the thesis of this chapter. This time, however, the new verse form is women community college presidents. Quite pointedly, my thesis is this: by connecting the characteristic strengths of their gender to the power of their office, women who are community college presidents have a golden opportunity to make a unique contribution to their institutions and society as a whole. They are what is happening to today's community college. They are indeed its new verse form, and their success in realizing the possibilities and meeting the challenges of their office has ramifications for society at large. This chapter explores the multiple connections among the multiple realities of this thesis by portraying the current status of women in the presidency, defining the leadership characteristics of women presidents, connecting these characteristics to a clarion call for new executive leadership, relating this call to the community college presidency, and proposing a framework for women presidents to effect meaningful institutional change and impact the larger public policy issues of academe and society at large.

Status of Women in the Presidency

Without question, women have made significant progress in attaining presidencies in American two-year and four-year institutions. According to the American Council on Education's most recent published analysis of women chief executive officers ("More Women Leading Higher Education Institutions," 1992, p. 1), 348, or 12 percent of the 3,000-plus chief executive officers (CEOs) employed in academe are women. This figure represents a 135 percent increase in the number of women CEOs heading American collegiate institutions between 1975 and 1992. An informal analysis of a March 19, 1993, ACE roster of women CEOs suggests that the trend, although slowing down, is continuing. As of that date, 379, or 12.6 percent of the CEOs were women.

Although increases are found in all types of institutions, they are especially significant in the two-year public sector. Of the 348 women CEOs in 1992, 136, or 39 percent headed two-year institutions and, of these, 77.9 percent were in the public sector. The 1993 roster puts the figure at 153, or 40.4 percent, with 81.7 percent in the public sector.

The point is that two-year colleges appear to be at the forefront in placing women in their presidencies. The question is why. On the one hand, one might expect the community college to be the pacesetter in hiring women presidents. Since its founding, it has been hailed as the "people's college," "democracy's college," and "opportunity's college." With women over half its student body, it demonstrates a strong commitment to the values of open access, diversity, and inclusiveness. On the other hand, the steadily rising number of women presidents in the community college may simply be a result of the institution's lower hierarchical status in academe. Put less diplomatically, the community college is at the bottom of the power rung anyway; why not leave the messy business of women CEOs to it?

Interestingly, women CEOs at the senior institutional level inadvertently give some credence to the latter explanation. In a 1991 news story in the *Chronicle of Higher Education,* several women CEOs were interviewed on the status of women presidents (Leatherman, 1991). They agreed that women have made considerable strides in the presidential arena; however, they also agreed that women have had less opportunity for the "plum leadership jobs" and are often left in the position of "tak[ing] on the presidency at a troubled institution, or be[ing] offered none at all" (Leatherman, 1991, p. A19). Said Paula Brownlee, the former president of Hollins College, "There's no conspiracy about it. I think it is a matter of what are the alternative options for the women versus the alternative options for the men. I suspect for women the range is not as great" (Leatherman, 1991, p. A19). What are the implications for the community college presidency? At the time of the news article, 41 percent of the 360 women CEOs were at two-year colleges (Leatherman, 1991, p. A20), yet no community college president was interviewed for the piece. One cannot help but speculate why.

Regardless of reason, the connection between gender and power is difficult to miss. However, the community college offers the ideal setting for women presidents to provide the leadership to redefine the connection and, in so doing, to have a positive impact on their institutions, the larger higher education community, and society as a whole.

Leadership Characteristics of Women Presidents

"If we had a keen vision and feeling of all ordinary human life, it would be like hearing the grass grow and the squirrel's heart beat, and we should die of that roar which lies on the other side of silence" (G. Eliot, 1872, p. 189). Most versed in women's studies recognize these words as an oft-quoted excerpt from George Eliot's *Middlemarch* (1872). For purposes here, they are a powerful context for an analysis of the leadership characteristics of women presidents. Indeed these characteristics are rooted deeply in Eliot's "other side of silence."

Carol Gilligan's *In a Different Voice* (1982) does an excellent job of penetrating this "other side." Gilligan traces the development of women's morality to notions of responsibility and care. She contends there is a difference between men's and women's decision-making and judgment calls. For women, she argues, there is less likely to be a sense of "blind justice" that relies on abstract laws and absolute impartiality. Instead, women tend to have a context of moral choice which acknowledges both that the needs of individuals cannot always be deduced from general rules and principles and that moral choice must be determined inductively from the particular experiences each participant brings to the situation. In contrast to the male vision of a hierarchy of power, women view the world as a web of relationships.

Others have amplified on Gilligan's work. Belenky, Clinchy, Goldberger, and Tarule (1986) take Gilligan's idea of moral choice for women and identify what they call "women's ways of knowing." They claim that women come to know through silence, through listening to the voices of others, through the quest for self, through the voice of reason, and through connecting all of the above. Josselson (1987) takes Gilligan's sense of self and suggests it affects women's individual approaches to forming relationships, making decisions about family and children, pursuing careers, developing religious beliefs and worldviews, and more. And, in her rather provocative book, *The Female World,* Bernard (1981) provides a comprehensive study of the female ethos, concluding the female world is based on an ethos of love and duty whereas the male world is based on an ethos of power and competition. For all, the notion of interconnectedness holds a paramount place in women's reasoning structures.

Finding the roar to this "other side of silence" has led to a plethora of research which strongly supports the notion that women's leadership styles differ from men's. Rosener (1990) studied men and women executives with similar backgrounds and concluded that the way they managed was different. Rosener found men to lead through a series of what she calls "transactions," rewarding employees for a job well done and punishing them for a job poorly done. She found women leaders more interested in transforming people's self-interest into organizational goals, with the women being quick to encourage participation, share power and information, enhance other people's self-worth, and get others excited about their work.

"The Web" Versus "The Pyramid." Helgesen's work (1990a) paints a similar picture. Helgesen conducted an in-depth study of four women executives and found them to be successful precisely because they did not follow what some might call the more traditional (male) model of management. For example, they freely exhibited and used such stereotypically female strengths as supporting, encouraging and teaching, soliciting input, and, in general, creating a positive, collegial work environment. As Helgesen puts it, women leaders like being "in the center of things, rather than at the top, which they perceived as a lonely and disconnected position" (Helgesen, 1990a, p. 44). Consequently, they often avoid traditional hierarchies in favor of "circular management," metaphorically being a part of "the web" rather than "the pyramid" (Helgesen, 1990b, p. F13).

"Women's Leadership." Numerous other studies done over the past several years have led to similar conclusions. However, the surest sign that the differences in women's and men's leadership styles have become institutionalized is the special billing they receive in Aburdene and Naisbitt's *Megatrends for Women* (1992). Aburdene and Naisbitt coined the term "women's leadership" to describe what they consider to be a leadership personality that reflects "women's values" and subsequently translates them into "leadership behavior" (p. 89).

Specifically, they identify 25 leadership behaviors and cluster them into six central traits as follows:

Empower. Women "reward" rather than "punish," "invite speaking out" rather than "demand respect," are "motivators" rather than "drill sergeants," "value creativity" rather than "impose discipline," are interested in "vision" rather than the "bottom line."

Restructure. Women seek to "change" rather than "control," "connect" rather than "rank," establish a "network" rather than a "hierarchy." They are "holistic" and "systemic" rather than "mechanistic" and "compartmental." They are "flexible" rather than "rigid."

Teaching. Women "facilitate" rather than "give orders." They prefer the "teaching archetype" to the "military archetype."

Role Model. Women "act as role models"; they do not "issue orders."

Openness. Women cultivate a "nourishing environment for growth." They "reach out" rather than up or down. They advocate "information availability" rather than "information control."

Questioner. Women "ask the right questions" rather than "know all the answers." [Aburdene and Naisbitt, 1992, p. 91]

So how well does this research depict the leadership characteristics of women who are community college presidents? According to the work of Gillett-Karam

(1994), it reflects them quite well. Gillett-Karam attempted to see to what extent (if any) five cluster dimensions of transformational leadership—namely, vision, people orientation, motivation orientation, empowerment, and values orientation—were gender based. Although she found the general clusters as a whole were not gender based, four "separate behaviors" within the clusters were significantly higher for women and two were significantly higher for men. The "feminine" behaviors were as follows: "(1) risk taking or taking appropriate risks to bring about change, a *vision* behavior; (2) demonstrates caring and respect for individual differences, a *people* behavior; (3) acts collaboratively, an *influence* behavior; and (4) builds openness and trust, a *values* behavior" (Gillett-Karam, 1994, p. 103).

The "masculine" behaviors were as follows: "(1) rewards others contingent on their effort and performance, a *people* behavior; and (2) is characterized by a bias for action, an *influence* behavior" (Gillett-Karam, 1994, p. 103).

In short, Gillett-Karam's findings corroborate the more general research conducted on women executives. They also characterize a recent group of impressive dissertation studies on women community college presidents (Adams, 1993; Guill, 1991; Mennuti, 1987; Miles, 1986; Sanders, 1990; Schmidt, 1990), which collectively lends further credence to Aburdene and Naisbitt's (1992) model of women's leadership. Suffice it to say that George Eliot's "other side of silence" is silent no more. Clearly women are beginning to redefine the power structure by redefining what constitutes effective leadership.

Clarion Call for New Executive Leadership

The New Paradigm. In virtually all fields of knowledge, researchers have begun to define a shift in the way the world operates. They refer to it as the "new paradigm." This new paradigm is characterized by a "world ordered by heterarchy" not hierarchy, with information and authority flowing across channels and input from all members of a defined entity considered valid and important (Lincoln, 1985, p. 34). It is "holographic" and "perspectival" rather than "mechanical" and "objective" (Kuh, Whitt, and Shedd, 1987, pp. 14, 23). It defines the world less in terms of "linear causality" where there is a direct connection between an action and its outcomes and more in terms of "mutual causality . . . where A and B cannot be separated into simple cause-effect relationships" (Schwartz and Ogilvy, 1979, p. 14). With this new paradigm has come a clarion call for new executive leadership. The call is resounding in both the business world and academe. It is being answered with a new leadership that manifests many of the leadership characteristics distinctly labeled as "feminine."

Framing the New Leadership. Of particular use in defining the new leadership is the recent work of Bolman and Deal (1991) on reframing organizations. Bolman and Deal developed a model for "integrated leadership" within the context of four situational frames. The frames are *structural,* where the leader analyzes and designs as the "social architect"; *human resource,* where the leader supports and empowers as the "catalyst or servant"; *political,* where the leader advocates and builds coalitions as the "advocate"; and *symbolic,* where the leader inspires and frames the experience as "prophet or poet" (Bolman and Deal, 1991, pp. 423–445). Bolman and Deal contend that the effective leader is comfortable moving in and out of the frames as the situation demands.

Interestingly, the four frames resonate the roar of women from the "other side of silence." For example, they adopt (inadvertently, no doubt) Gilligan's (1982) notion of responsibility and care, giving decision making a context of moral choice. They also place the effective leader in Helgesen's (1990) web, in the center of things organizationally rather than on top of the hierarchical pyramid.

Corporate Quest for New Leadership. Adaptations of women's leadership are especially evident in the corporate world's call for new executive leadership. From its many perspectives (Guest, 1986; Kanter, 1989; Zaleznik, 1989), this new executive leadership also resonates "the other side of silence." It reflects Bernard's (1981) ethos of love and duty as well as Aburdene and Naisbitt's (1992) emphasis on empowerment, restructuring, teaching, role modeling, openness, and questioning. It also has the transformational elements of Gillett-Karam's (1994) "feminine" behaviors—namely, caring and respect, risk taking, collaboration, and openness and trust. Suffice it to say that what was once called a woman's leadership style in the twentieth century has now become the new leadership for the twenty-first century.

The New Executive Leadership and the Community College Presidency

What then are the implications of this new leadership for those who lead community colleges? In his landmark study of the community college presidency, Vaughan (1986) notes that the role of the community college president has undergone a dramatic metamorphosis over the last thirty years as community colleges themselves have changed. The ideal profile of the community college president today embraces the leadership characteristics defined earlier in this chapter as belonging to the new leadership for the twenty-first century. Indeed, recent studies of community college CEOs draw from a common lexicon to describe the effective executive leader. The lexicon includes descriptors like "facilitator," "social convener," "interdependence," "inclusiveness," "collaboration," "visionary," "high energy," "risk taking," "openness," "human relation interactional skills," "trustworthy," "motivator," and "flexibility," (Duncan and Harlacher, 1991; Vaughan, Mellander, and Blois, 1994). One professional journal ("More Women Leading Higher Education Institutions," 1991) even featured the elegant photograph of a symphony conductor on its cover to illustrate the "leadership for the new millennium" (p. 1). Given the edge that women who are community college presidents have on this new leadership, they are well positioned to make unique contributions to their institutions and society as a whole.

Framework for Action

And what exactly are these contributions? Exactly how should these women presidents proceed? I propose the following actions as a blueprint for those who are women community college presidents to effect meaningful change at their institutions and impact larger public policy issues of academe and society at large. Of course, although the elaborations of each action are focused specifically on women presidents, the general actions are useful ones for men presidents also.

Initially break down institutional gender stereotypes. For obvious reasons, most women who enter the community college presidency do so making history for their respective institutions. In other words, as they assume the presidency, they forever break the gender barrier at their institutions, creating a new "first" for the institution and often for the larger community the college serves. Above all else, women presidents must embrace the powerful symbol of the moment. And they must recognize the reality that not everyone inside and outside the institution is bursting with joy over their presidential appointment; in fact, there is most likely a bet or two riding on how long the new first will last. Nonetheless, carpe diem! Through the symbolic power of their office, women presidents can break down institutional gender stereotypes to the benefit of all faculty, staff, and students.

Penetrate institution's power structure and redefine its sense of power. Women can also use the power of their office to affect their institutions' power structures and, in so doing, to create institutional climates conducive to a collective redefining of power. Most institutions have at least some form of a "good old boy" network. They also have a collection of self-identified people who qualify only for membership in the institution's disenfranchised club. Neither the network nor the disenfranchised group hail exclusively from one gender, one ethnic background, one anything. Yet the former tends to exhibit predominantly "masculine" behavior and the latter predominantly "feminine" behavior. The opportunity (and challenge) that women presidents have is to redefine the institutional structure which gives life to both entities.

Although the best strategy for doing so is clearly individual to the institution and its culture, some obvious places to look include the institution's overall governance structure, its process for appointments to important committees, its promotion and tenure policy and practices, its recruitment and hiring policy and practices, and its salary structure. Women presidents are also well positioned to model a power structure built less on hierarchy and more on relationship, with a free exchange of information and an openness for collegial debate and discussion. They can be mentors for women faculty and staff and role models for women students. In short, through the strengths of their gender and the power of their office, women presidents can "find the voice of their reluctant followers" (Couto, 1993, p. 1) and make it the voice of a redefined sense of institutional power.

Use power of office to alter gender-related institutional policy. No community college is an island. In the most fundamental sense, community colleges are a microcosm of society at large and, as such, mirror the good and bad of that society. Sexual misconduct is a very real societal bad; yet it is often given only lip service at the people's colleges. Women community college presidents are uniquely positioned to ensure that their institutions adopt and enforce strong policies on sexual assault and sexual harassment. They can use the power of their office to "heighten [the] awareness of the need and create opportunities for [the full college community] to develop a stronger global perspective. . .[and] to foster a deeper understanding of violence in all its forms" (American Council on Education, 1994, p. 7). In short, they can use it to build community for the brave new world of a new century and its community colleges.

Raise collegial consciousness and initiate collegial dialogue on gender and related issues. The roar of George Eliot's "other side of silence" is alive and well on today's community college campuses. It is filled with the deafening silence of often painful collegial memories and manifests itself in isolated events of gender and related matters long ago swept under the rug institutionally. It yearns to be heard but has, for too long, thought it really had no voice. It has many reluctant followers—some men, some women; some people of color, some white; some homosexual, some heterosexual. It spans the breadth and depth of the institution's being, covering such topical areas as campus civility, multicultural diversity, collegial power, equal opportunity, and conflict resolution. Simply put, women community college presidents can use the power of their office and the strengths of their gender to give this "silence" an institutional voice.

Become an active player for public policy development and debate beyond the college level. At the 1990 ACE Women Presidents' Summit, Johnetta Cole, president of Spelman College, evoked the words of the abolitionist and suffragist Sojourner Truth: "Now if one woman in one garden was said to turn the world upside down, surely all of these womenfolk here can turn it right side up again" (Blum, 1990, p. A15). Here, in large measure, lies the ultimate challenge and opportunity for women community college presidents—to somehow turn the world "right side up again." In other words, women community college presidents can contribute to society's larger agendas by becoming active players for public policy development and debate in the regional, state, and national arenas.

In 1994 ACE's Office of Women in Higher Education published *A Blueprint for Leadership: How Women College and University Presidents Can Shape the Future.* An outgrowth of the 1993 ACE Women Presidents' Summit, this document articulated the vision for the involvement of the higher education woman executive in matters beyond her campus. As such, it has a particular relevance for women presidents in the community college. The document outlines three broad areas in which women CEOs should become involved, namely, redefinitions of war and peace, the economy and environment, and the intersection of public and private life. However, the defined areas of involvement and specific ways to be involved are of far less importance than the rallying call for involvement. As the new leadership for democracy's colleges, women community college presidents must answer this call.

Conclusion: A Call to Action

T. S. Eliot is really quite correct: "Few things that can happen to a nation are more important than the invention of a new form of verse" (1927, p. xii). For the community college, that new verse form is women community college presidents. To be sure, the challenges facing this new invention are immense but the opportunities are equally so. May those who lead answer the call to action. Society at large shall indeed be the ultimate beneficiary.

References

Aburdene, P., and Naisbitt, J. *Megatrends for Women.* New York: Villard Books, 1992.

Adams, C. "Leadership Characteristics of Four Community College Women Presidents: A Case Study." Unpublished doctoral dissertation, Colorado State University, 1993.

American Council on Education. *A Blueprint for Leadership: How Women College and University Presidents Can Shape the Future.* Washington, D.C.: American Council on Education, 1994.

Belenky, M., Clinchy, B., Goldberger, N., and Tarule, J. *Women's Ways of Knowing.* New York: Basic Books, 1986.

Bernard, J. *The Female World.* New York: Free Press, 1981.

Blum, D. "165 Female College Presidents 'Honor Progress, Connect with Each Other,' and Commiserate." *Chronicle of Higher Education,* Dec. 19, 1990, pp. A13, A14.

Bolman, L., and Deal, T. *Reframing Organizations.* San Francisco: Jossey-Bass, 1991.

Couto, R. "Leadership in the 21st Century: Finding the Voice of Reluctant Followers." Paper presented at the annual meeting of the Virginia Social Science Association, Lexington, Mar. 26, 1993.

Duncan, A., and Harlacher, E. "The Twenty-First Century Executive Leader." *Community College Review,* 1991, *18* (4), 39–47.

Eliot, G. *Middlemarch.* London: Penguin Books, 1872.

Eliot, T. S. *Shakespeare and the Stoicism of Seneca.* London: Oxford University Press, 1927.

Gillett-Karam, R. "Women and Leadership." In G. Baker (ed.), *A Handbook on the Community College in America.* Westport, Conn.: Greenwood Press, 1994.

Gilligan, C. *In a Different Voice.* Cambridge, Mass.: Harvard University Press, 1982.

Guest, R. "Management Imperatives for the Year 2000." *California Management Review,* 1986, *28* (4), 62–70.

Guill, J. "Conflict Management Style Preferences of Community College Presidents." Unpublished doctoral dissertation, University of Virginia, 1991.

Helgesen, S. *The Female Advantage: Women's Ways of Leadership.* New York: Doubleday Currency, 1990a.

Helgesen, S. "The Pyramid and the Web." *New York Times Forum,* May 27, 1990b, p. F13.

Josselson, R. *Finding Herself: Pathways to Identity Development in Women.* San Francisco: Jossey-Bass, 1987.

Kanter, R. "The New Managerial Work." *Harvard Business Review,* 1989, *67,* 85–92.

Kuh, G., Whitt, E., and Shedd, J. *Student Affairs Work 2001: A Paradigmatic Odyssey.* Alexandria, Va.: American College Personnel Association, 1987.

Leatherman, C. "Colleges Hire More Female Presidents, But Questions Linger About Their Clout." *Chronicle of Higher Education,* Nov. 6, 1991, pp. A19–A21.

Lincoln, Y. *Organizational Theory and Inquiry.* Newbury Park, Calif.: Sage, 1985.

Mennuti, R. "An Exploration of Moral Orientation, Gender and the Nature of the Dilemma in Moral Reasoning of Community College Presidents." Unpublished doctoral dissertation, Virginia Polytechnic Institute and State University, 1987.

Miles, K. "A Naturalistic Inquiry into the Administrative Behavior of a Top-Level Woman Executive in a Two-Year College." Unpublished doctoral dissertation, University of Colorado, Boulder, 1986.

"More Women Leading Higher Education Institutions." *Higher Education & National Affairs,* June 8, 1992, pp. 1, 3.

Rosener, J. "Ways Women Lead." *Harvard Business Review,* 1990, *68,* 119–125.

Sanders, S. "A Profile of Experienced Women Chief Executive Officers of Two-Year Colleges." Unpublished doctoral dissertation, University of Arkansas, 1989.

Schmidt, M. "Gender Balance and Leadership: A Study of Community College Presidents' Leadership Described in Gender Related Terms." Unpublished doctoral dissertation, Seattle University, 1990.

Schwartz, P., and Ogilvy, J. *The Emergent Paradigm.* Analytical Report no. 7, Values and Lifestyles Program. Menlo Park, Calif.: SRI International, 1979.

Vaughan, G., Mellander, G., and Blois, B. *The Community College Presidency.* New York: Macmillan, 1986.

Vaughan, G., Mellander, G., and Blois, B. *The Community College Presidency: Current Status and Future Outlook.* Washington, D.C.: American Association of Community Colleges, 1994.

Zaleznik, A. *The Managerial Mystique: Restoring Leadership in Business.* New York: HarperCollins, 1989.

DEBORAH M. DICROCE is president of Piedmont Virginia Community College in Charlottesville.

INDEX

Ordering Information

NEW DIRECTIONS FOR COMMUNITY COLLEGES is a series of paperback books that provides expert assistance to help community colleges meet the challenges of their distinctive and expanding educational mission. Books in the series are published quarterly in Spring, Summer, Fall, and Winter and are available for purchase by subscription and individually.

SUBSCRIPTIONS for 1995 cost $49.00 for individuals (a savings of more than 25 percent over single-copy prices) and $72.00 for institutions, agencies, and libraries. Please do not send institutional checks for personal subscriptions. Standing orders are accepted.

SINGLE COPIES cost $16.95 when payment accompanies order. (California, New Jersey, New York, and Washington, D.C., residents please include appropriate sales tax.) All orders will be charged postage and handling.

DISCOUNTS FOR QUANTITY ORDERS are available. Please write to the address below for information.

ALL ORDERS must include either the name of an individual or an official purchase order number. Please submit your order as follows:
   Subscriptions: specify series and year subscription is to begin
   Single copies: include individual title code (such as CC82)

MAIL ALL ORDERS TO:
   Jossey-Bass Publishers
   350 Sansome Street
   San Francisco, California 94104-1342

FOR SUBSCRIPTION SALES OUTSIDE OF THE UNITED STATES, contact any international subscription agency or Jossey-Bass directly.

OTHER TITLES AVAILABLE IN THE
NEW DIRECTIONS FOR COMMUNITY COLLEGES SERIES
Arthur M. Cohen, Editor-in-Chief
Florence B. Brawer, Associate Editor

CC88   Assessment and Testing: Myths and Realities, *Trudy H. Bers, Mary L. Mitller*
CC87   Creating and Maintaining a Diverse Faculty, *William B. Harvey, James Valadez*
CC86   Relating Curriculum and Transfer, *Arthur M. Cohen*
CC85   A Practical Guide to Conducting Customized Work Force Training, *Sherrie L. Kantor*
CC84   Changing Managerial Imperatives, *Richard L. Alfred, Patricia Carter*
CC83   Accreditation of the Two-Year College, *Carolyn Prager*
CC82   Academic Advising: Organizing and Delivering Services for Student Success, *Margaret C. King*
CC81   Directing General Education Outcomes, *Neal A. Raisman*
CC80   First Generation Students: Confronting the Cultural Issues, *L. Steven Zwerling, Howard B. London*
CC79   Maintaining Faculty Excellence, *Keith Kroll*
CC78   Prisoners of Elitism: The Community College's Struggle for Stature, *Billie Wright Dziech, William R. Vilter*
CC77   Critical Thinking: Educational Imperative, *Cynthia A. Barnes*
CC73   Writing Across the Curriculum in Community Colleges, *Linda C. Stanley, Joanna Ambron*
CC71   The Role of the Learning Resource Center in Instruction, *Margaret Holleman*
CC70   Developing International Education Programs, *Richard K. Greenfield*
CC63   Collaborating with High Schools, *Janet E. Lieberman*
CC59   Issues in Student Assessment, *Dorothy Bray, Marcia J. Belcher*
CC58   Developing Occupational Programs, *Charles R. Doty*